50 Strategies for Communicating and Working with Diverse Families

Third Edition

JANET GONZALEZ-MENA
Beginning Together

PEARSON

Boston   Columbus   Indianapolis   New York   San Francisco   Upper Saddle River
Amsterdam   Cape Town   Dubai   London   Madrid   Milan   Munich   Paris   Montréal
Toronto   Delhi   Mexico City   São Paulo   Sydney   Hong Kong   Seoul   Singapore   Taipei   Tokyo

Vice President and Editorial
  Director: Jeffery W. Johnston
Senior Acquisitions Editor: Julie Peters
Editorial Assistant: Andrea Hall
Vice President, Director
  of Marketing: Margaret Waples
Senior Marketing Manager: Christopher Barry
Senior Managing Editor: Pamela D. Bennett
Project Manager: Kerry Rubadue
Production Manager: Laura Messerly

Senior Art Director: Jayne Conte
Cover Designer: Suzanne Behnke
Cover Image: © popocorn8/Fotolia
Full-Service Project
  Management: Hema Latha
Composition: Integra Software
  Services, Ltd
Printer/Binder: LSC Communications
Cover Printer: LSC Communications
Text Font: 10/12, Meridien LT Std

Credits and acknowledgments for materials borrowed from other sources and reproduced, with permission, in this textbook appear on the appropriate page within the text.

Photo Credits: AnastasiiaMarkus/Shutterstock, **p. 22**; Anton Gvozdikov/Fotolia, **p. 107**; Artur Golbert/Fotolia, **p. 135**; Artyom Yefimov/Fotolia, **p. 29**; auremar/Shutterstock, **p. 18**; Blend Images/Shutterstock, **p. 28**; CandyBox Images/Fotolia, **p. 97**; denys kuvaiev/Fotolia, **p. 68**; dubova/Fotolia, **p. 15**; Frank Gonzalez-Mena, **pp. 2, 17, 20, 25, 34, 36, 44, 50, 58, 77, 86, 89, 93, 126, 128** (both); Golden Pixels LLC/Shutterstock, **p. 111**; gpalmer/Fotolia, **p. 148**; Igor Normann/Shutterstock, **p. 63**; Ilike/Fotolia, **p. 60**; Iurii Sokolov/Fotolia, **p. 53**; Jaren Wicklund/Fotolia, **p. 9**; mangostock/Fotolia, **pp. 84, 150**; Marion Cowee, **p. 11**; matka Wariatka/Fotolia, **p.71**; michaeljung/Fotolia, **p. 119**; micromonkey/Fotolia, **p. 74**; Monkey Business/Fotolia, **pp. 131, 142**; Radoslaw Korga/Fotolia, **p. 145**; sonya etchison/Fotolia, **p. 104**; Tatyana Gladskih/Fotolia, **p. 140**; Tim Mena, **pp. 6, 40, 91**; WavebreakmediaMicro/Fotolia, **p. 138**; Yuri Arcurs/Fotolia, **p. 100**

Every effort has been made to provide accurate and current Internet information in this book. However, the Internet and information posted on it are constantly changing, so it is inevitable that some of the Internet addresses listed in this textbook will change.

Library of Congress Cataloging-in-Publication Data
Gonzalez-Mena, Janet.
  50 strategies for communicating and working with diverse families/Janet Gonzalez-Mena. —3rd ed.
    p. cm.
  Includes bibliographical references and index.
  ISBN-13: 978-0-13-309027-7
  ISBN-10: 0-13-309027-2
  1. Children—Services for—United States. 2. Early childhood education—United States.
  3. Family services—United States. 4. Multiculturalism—United States. I. Title. II. Title:
  Fifty strategies for communicating and working with diverse families.
  HV741.G637 2014
  362.70973—dc23

2012034135

ISBN 10:   0-13-309027-2
ISBN 13: 978-0-13-309027-7

Introduction

. . . .

This practical book provides strategies on honoring diversity and partnering with families to support, enhance, and maximize the quality of care and education of young children. Many of the strategies in this book address ideas about how early childhood professionals can create a climate of trust by communicating with family members in a collaborative way. The goal is to create useful, inclusive programs that respect and honor differences in families and individuals. These easy-to-use strategies provide a strong basis for working and communicating productively with families of all types and from varied backgrounds.

NEW IN THIS EDITION

- The third edition of this book addresses diversity up front in the first section, where chapter titles show a number of different types of families with whom readers will likely work. Though not all the chapter titles throughout the book necessarily reflect diversity, there is something about diversity in each one. The book has always been about diversity, but that fact was not always pointed out in each chapter of the first two editions. Now it is, with new sections added relating the subject matter of the chapter directly to diversity.

- An emphasis on antibias environments throughout helps the reader keep in mind that particular way of honoring differences.

- In keeping up with the times, this new edition is expanded to include military families and grandparents raising their grandchildren.

- With electronic media expanding every day, this edition helps the reader to reflect on the growing influence all types of media have on young children—even infants and toddlers.

- The book still addresses all levels of early education, from birth to eight years old, but in this new edition there is more focus on the reader who is concerned with the primary grades than in previous editions.

- The reader will find more about the influence of economic hardship on children and families, as more and more families now live in poverty.

- Changes in the sections called *What Teachers Can Do* include turning negatives into positives when strategies had previously included words like "don't." Also in those sections, additional strategies were added to almost every chapter.

- Stories, examples, and vignettes help readers to apply the information to real life, so those have been increased in this edition.

- This book has always asked the reader to use self-reflection as an important tool to understanding and working with families. This edition has increased that emphasis.

- At the request of reviewers, more on home visits was added, so even those readers who are or will end up in situations where they can't make home visits, will come to appreciate them.
- Some chapters, such as Chapter 40 on Transitions, have added material. That subject has been greatly expanded to give information and strategies related to more kinds of transitions so readers can move beyond ideas only about developmental transitions or changing classrooms or programs.

FAMILY-CENTERED CARE AND EDUCATION

This book is based on the concept called *family-centered care and education*. The tendency in the early care and education field in the past has been to focus on the child, and indeed, some programs actually used to use the words "child-centered programs" in their philosophy statements. This book is based on the idea that you can't separate the child from the context of the family. *The child* is a term that has no real meaning, because no child stands alone; the influences of the family are always present. When readers understand programs that regard those influences as a good thing, they are on their way to becoming family-centered. When a program becomes family-centered, diversity is a part of the package. Students of Early Childhood theories and practices will see that respecting diversity is addressed in two major sections and is an underpinning of all of the strategies. Where respecting diversity isn't boldly highlighted, it is still mentioned. With diversity comes the idea of equity as well as inclusion, meaning that early childhood educators have to be fair and include everybody. Educators can't celebrate diversity and then exclude some families from the program because they or their children are too *different*. This book is about including *all* families and their children. It's about honoring diversity, even when it is hard to do so.

WHAT DOES "PARTNERSHIP" REALLY MEAN?

Partnership is another theme in this book. In building partnerships, readers are shown that establishing trust is key because you can't have a partnership without it. A partnership is different from merely trying to get families to cooperate with the program and carry out its goals. Involving parents is an approach often taken with that idea in mind. Policymakers learn about how school readiness and academic achievement are strengthened when parents are involved in their children's education. They jump on the bandwagon to teach parents how to help their children carry out the program goals. The parents then learn how to help their children according to the school's way of doing things.

A partnership is different from that kind of parental involvement, because it implies equity and shared power rather than one side dominating the other. In a partnership, roles and responsibilities may differ, but both sides have rights. At the heart of the partnership lies the welfare of the child. Each partner—family member and teacher—brings different strengths and skills to the union. Partners collaborate rather than issue orders. In a partnership, communication is two-way rather than hierarchical. It takes communication skills for two parties to work in partnership. Accordingly, many of the strategies in this book relate to communication. Communication may be very different if the focus of the school is merely about getting parents on board so that they can help their children by doing at home what the school system and educators see as beneficial to readiness or academic achievement.

TRANSFORMATIVE EDUCATION IS THE MODEL

An approach to involving parents is often linked with parent education programs. The partnership approach is not the same, even though both involvement and education may well be part of it. Certainly, families who are involved in a program are more likely to take their partnership role seriously. Also, early childhood education professionals have knowledge, experience, and expertise that parents can benefit from; at the same time, parents know their own children, goals, beliefs, values, family traditions, and culture better than anyone else. So the educational model here is *transformative education* rather than the traditional teacher–student, one-way educational approach.

Transformative education is defined as two people or groups coming together and interacting in such a way that both parties learn something and are changed for the better by the interaction.

SOLVING THE NAME DILEMMA

In writing this book, I was faced with the problem of what to call the adults who work in early childhood programs. This book takes in a wide sweep of early childhood and includes children from birth to age eight. Although all adults in these programs could be called *teachers*, some who work with the youngest children resist that term because they don't *teach*; they *care for*. Others who resist the term *teacher* think of themselves as facilitators of learning and prefer to call themselves *educators*. Still other adults who work with children in that age range work out of their homes, not in schools or centers, and call themselves *family child care providers*. Early childhood education is a complex field, and no one name works for everybody in it.

I also had to figure out a name for the early childhood programs themselves, which included all the different forms. A third-grade classroom with a teacher is different from an infant–toddler center with caregivers, yet both fit under the label *early childhood education*. A half-day preschool is different from a kindergarten and also from a full-day child care program, which is different from a hospital child care center that is open 24 hours a day to serve staff on all shifts.

CARE AND EDUCATION CAN NEVER BE SEPARATED

So what names did I use? I addressed the dilemma by changing *early childhood education* to *early care and education* and calling the adults who work in the field *teachers* at some times and *early care and education professionals* or *early childhood professionals* at other times. Adding the word *care* highlights the idea that care and education can never be separated in the early years. The letters ECE, which are commonly used to define the programs for children ages birth to age eight, are used by some to mean *Early Childhood Education*. I use those letters to mean *Early Care and Education* to broaden the scope. To me it is very important to link education with care, and not use the term education alone, even when the example is in a primary classroom in a public school.

For young children, care is always a part of the educational process. Nell Noddings writes about this subject in many books, and she takes in the whole realm of education when she says care must always be part of it—even through higher education. The point is that though you may separate programs by the age of the children they serve, and give them different labels, all should include both education and care.

Other terms also varied by the focus of the strategy, so sometimes I used *school* and *classroom*, and other times I used *program* and *center*. Sometimes I was aiming more at teachers in schools, and other times more at staff in programs such as prekindergarten or preschool, infant–toddler programs, early intervention programs, child care, Head Start, Early Head Start, and school-age child care. It's complex, because these programs take place in a variety of environments, including centers, schools, and homes, and some strategies pertain more to one setting than to the others.

In summary, this book is a targeted text that offers practical strategies for partnering with families, creating the trust necessary for true collaboration, and developing programs that include all families and individuals. Of course, at the heart of all these useful strategies lies the welfare of the child.

ACKNOWLEDGMENTS

I would like to thank the following people for helping make this book what it is: Marion Cowee, Lynne Doherty Lyle, Tim Gonzalez-Mena, Lisa Lee, Kitty Ritz, Ethel Seiderman, and Joan Symonds. In addition, I wish to thank the following reviewers for their suggestions and insights: Elizabeth Kirby Fullerton, University of North Florida; Lisa M. Lauer, Nicholls State University; Anne Leser, Bowling Green State University; and Michelle Mallory, Clark College.

Contents

1 Appreciating All Kinds of Families

· ·

WHAT TEACHERS NEED TO KNOW

Families vary in income levels. They also come in many sizes, shapes, structures, and configurations. For example, there are two-parent families, single-parent families, and extended families with several generations in one household. There are stepfamilies and blended families, biracial families, gay families, and straight families. Grandparents may be raising their grandchildren, or older siblings raising younger ones. Transnational families may live in two countries. Migrant families may move where the work is. Military families may move a lot and/or experience periods of separation. Children may have been born into the family or come by other means, such as foster care, adoptions, or kinship networks. Some children live in more than one home and are members of more than one family.

There are many definitions of *family*. Those definitions may focus on genetics, residence, emotional ties, rules, or legal status. The American Academy of Family Physicians (2003) defines family as "a group of individuals with a continuing legal, genetic, and/ or emotional relationship." One teacher defines family as "the people living in the children's homes who love and care for them," and this same teacher also makes sure that all families are welcomed and respected (Rieger, 2008). She lets children and their families know that if they care to, they can talk about family members who may not be with them, recognizing that military duty, divorce, incarceration, and death can separate family members from the child.

Not all families have homes. The general view of the homeless population may be of city-dwelling, single adult men with mental illness or alcohol or drug additions, but the truth is that homeless families are everywhere and many of them have children. This group needs the same respect and consideration as any other group of families and often needs more support and services than most families in the school or other early childhood setting. Homelessness disrupts every aspect of family life, including the health and well-being of the members and the education of their children (Thoennes, 2008).

In a workshop, Linda Brault (2007) asked participants to categorize their families in terms of size by raising their hands when she asked, "How many grew up in a large family? A small family? A medium-sized family?" There was wide disparity in their concept of large, small, and medium-sized families. Some counted only their parents and siblings. Others counted extended family members. When the presenter questioned individuals further, it became clear they had very different definitions of families and membership in them. For example, some counted dead people as family members and deemed them as important as live family members. For other participants, nonrelatives had the same status as blood relatives. This was a racially, ethnically, and culturally diverse group, which showed the many different concepts about who makes up a *family*.

One of the problems in working with diverse families arises when the teacher's notion of family gets in the way of understanding and respecting all kinds of families. The problem is magnified when a family who doesn't live up to the teacher's picture of an ideal family is suspected of child abuse, while the same teacher overlooks signs of abuse in an "ideal" family. Since teachers and other early childhood professionals are mandated reporters, the repercussions could be serious, not only for the children and the families but also for the teacher.

While looking at all the different kinds of families that teachers and other early educators can work with, recent immigrants are in a special category. Immigrant status may have a huge influence on how the family operates. It's important to recognize that all Americans, except for Native Americans, were once immigrants. It's also important to realize that at one time or another most immigrant groups have been blamed for the woes of the nation. Some immigrant families face a good deal of prejudice in addition to the other challenges facing them as they settle in a country that is different from the one in which they were born. Early care and education programs should support these families and do what they can to help them deal with their many challenges.

WHAT TEACHERS CAN DO

- Start by putting aside the idea of a "normal" or "ideal" family. Broaden your definition of family. When you approach a family who doesn't fit your ideal, you see them as "other," and "othering" people gets in the way of getting to know them and building a relationship. For many, the ideal family consists of a mother, father, two children, and maybe a dog, who all live together enjoying a middle-class lifestyle. That's one kind of family—there are many others!

- Realize that families who don't fit common notions of normal or ideal have to deal with being stereotyped, discriminated against, or ignored. Even though research on stereotypes is increasing, much of it focuses on race, gender, income level, and religion more than on changing the stigmas attached to families who vary from what is considered "the norm."

- Recognize that teachers must value all families and move away from stereotypes and preconceived ideas about different kinds of families.

- Examine your program and institution to shed light on how the curriculum, materials, administrative hiring practices, and policies teach children and parents lessons about values related to families. The goal should be for all families to receive the same respect.

Teachers must value all families and move away from stereotypes and preconceived ideas.

- If you have family figures for a dollhouse or block area, put them all in one container, and let children decide for themselves how they want to configure a family. Don't set them up the way they came, with matching mother, father, and children.
- Learn to communicate and build relationships with people who are different from yourself, and become aware of the pitfalls of miscommunication.
- Be aware of the kinds of activities and assignments that relate to the child's family or the family's history, which may be painful, unavailable, or unknown. Asking about the origin of a child's name or for baby pictures can be a problem for children who were adopted past infancy. Asking a family to share artifacts can be painful if they fled from their homeland with only the clothes on their backs.
- Instead of celebrating Mother's Day or Father's Day as such, create a celebration day for children to show their gratitude for the person or persons who care for them. Let the child choose the person or persons to honor. Mother's Day or Father's Day can be painful for some single-parent or gay and lesbian families.
- Use a variety of means for contacting, working with, and involving family members in their children's out-of-home education and care.
- Get families involved with each other, and create a community.
- Recognize that the teacher has a good deal to learn from families—teaching should be regarded as a two-way process, which can be called a teaching–learning process, where the teacher and the learner often trade places.

2 Working with Immigrant Families

Newly arrived immigrant families have a good many challenges. If they arrive undocumented (without papers) they may have fears that documented immigrants don't have. Will a family member be "picked up" and incarcerated? Will children be left behind when family members are deported? Will young family members who have no memories of the old country end up back there alone, without the language or skills to get along? The newspapers tell heart-rending immigrant stories. Although any immigrant may face bias and discrimination, some face much more than others.

Language can be a huge challenge for immigrants. At a time when new arrivals have so many new things to learn, their communication system may be compromised. All the change of leaving the old behind and starting new in a strange culture brings stress. Language difficulties greatly add to the stress. Nothing is easy, and immigrants meet up with intolerant people while they are getting settled—finding a place to live, signing up for utilities, understanding the transportation system, and getting a new job. When people can't understand immigrants, they sometimes get impatient with them. In a new language and culture, immigrants are slower than in their old country. They make many mistakes and sometimes are regarded as ignorant; however, if you could see them operate in their own language and familiar surroundings, they aren't the same people!

At a time when they need support, many immigrants are on their own. They have had to leave their support networks, including the extended family, behind. They may be alone in the world for the first time in their lives.

After immigrants have been here a while, the children in the family often get ahead of the adults in learning the language and figuring out the new ways of the society they live in. That situation puts parents at a huge disadvantage because traditional roles are reversed. Now the children are the ones who know best. They may even be embarrassed by their parents' awkward ways, difficulties in communication, and their accents. Where respect for the authority of elders was once the rule, now the children are the authorities. What worries for a family! Discipline may no longer work, and the children may be largely on their own.

Even though families may be uncomfortable about what is happening to their children, they have to send them to school, which may be quite different from schools in their own country. Sometimes they are forced to put their children in out-of-home care. Grandma is no longer there to stay with them, and immigrants may be unhappy about turning their children over to nonfamily members in child care programs. They may worry about identity issues and that their children may become assimilated and lose their cultural ties.

Although sometimes immigrant families disagree with what they see in the school or other early care and education program, they may feel as if they are putting their children into the hands of those they consider to be the authority, especially if such a person is called *teacher* or *director*. "The professional knows best" is their attitude. These families may have great respect for authority.

Some families still see themselves as the authority at home; in their minds, they create a huge separation between what they do at home and what happens in the early childhood

This sign was on the wall of a kindergarten classroom to make families feel welcome by finding their own language displayed.

program. Other families grant the teacher or other early childhood education professional supreme authority over all things to do with children, both in the program and at home. They see their job as learning about it so that they can do the same at home. When one teacher told a family who recently immigrated from another country that they should speak English to their children at home, they followed her advice even though their ability to speak English was limited. The result was that parent-child communication was greatly limited, and everyone was frustrated for a long time. The parents' English improved, but they always had a heavy accent and never became truly articulate in that language as compared to their own. The children learned English from school and from their peers but, to their parents' great sorrow, lost their home language.

Alicia Lieberman, a mental health specialist, offers strategies for working with immigrant families in her classic article "Concerns of Immigrant Families" (1995). The strategies she suggests are included in those listed below.

WHAT TEACHERS CAN DO

- Appreciate the family's culture. Remember that difference doesn't mean deficit. Learn about the differences—is this a family where respect for elders means looking downward rather than looking them in the eye? You don't have to be an anthropologist to learn from families. Observation is one way; asking questions is another. Establish a relationship with each family so that asking questions doesn't put them on the defensive.

- If there is a language difference, remember to work with it. Talk as clearly as you can, using short sentences and plain words. Avoid jargon. Learn some words in the family's language and use them regularly.

- Make the classroom reflect the languages and cultures of the people in it, including the families and staff members. Appreciate and promote the home language of each family.

- Explain the routine of the program or classroom. Families may come from countries where the customs are very different.

- Acknowledge tension, and think about the reasons for it. Chances are that any tension between you and the parent is due to cultural differences.

- Ask parents about their child-rearing practices. When you don't understand a particular behavior or practice find out how things are done in their country. Try to communicate about your difference so that it's seen by the family as just that—a difference—and not as a deficiency on their part.

- Be aware of differing attitudes, practices, and perceptions of children and adults with disabilities.

- Serve as a cultural bridge between the parents' culture and the culture of the classroom or child care program. Help the parents understand the way things are done in the classroom or center.

- Remember that you are an authority figure and that most families want your approval.

- Establish a trusting atmosphere that encourages dialogue. Build trust before you try discussing problems, and when you do discuss problems, try to do so in ways that avoid a critical tone. Instead, express care and concern.

- Remember that immigration causes great stress for the whole family. People who felt self-confident and competent in their home country are now trying to learn some basic skills. They may be suffering from depression. But many immigrants with children in early care and education programs are full of hope for the future. You are part of that hope.

- Appreciate their culture, support them, and help them adjust to life in a new country.

Notice what is on the bulletin board under Broadway Children's School. How do you think immigrants feel when they find their own language in evidence around the classroom? That's one way of saying, "You are welcome here."

3 Including Families of Children with Special Needs

Classrooms and centers set up for typically developing children are now required by law to accept children with special needs. All children must be provided with care and education in the least restrictive setting where their typically developing peers are served. That law has provided benefits to everybody—not just to children and families with special needs. By making a program or school inclusive, everybody gains for the following reasons:

1 Diversity of all sorts is a bonus. Everybody benefits from being around people who are different from themselves—children and parents alike—especially if the early childhood professionals know how to help them appreciate differences and interact with each other in respectful ways.

2 Children with special needs benefit by being integrated with their typically developing peers instead of being segregated into special education programs. They learn to live in a world that has a greater variety of people in it than they would find in special education programs that are exclusively for them. Children who are developing typically also enjoy benefits by being around all kinds of people—not just those who are like themselves.

3 Teachers benefit by expanding their knowledge of how to meet a variety of needs, some of which they might not have encountered before they experienced inclusion.

4 Families who have children with special needs benefit from being integrated with families who have typically developing children and learning about them and their successes and challenges, just as those families with typically developing children benefit from learning about the successes and challenges of families of children with special needs.

WHAT TEACHERS CAN DO

- If parents of children who have special challenges or disabilities do not arrive in the classroom already acting as advocates for their children, encourage them to take on that role. They will need those skills as their children move on from your program or classroom to others. If they are already advocates, you need to appreciate that. You can learn a good deal from families and from the specialists with whom they are involved.

- Give emotional support to all families when needed. Recognize that families who have children with special needs or challenges may need even more support and understanding. Although many families have already had plenty of experience in coping with their emotions, others may be still at the stages of grieving that accompany the discovery that their child's development is not following a typical pathway. Feelings of anger, sadness, resentment, frustration, and guilt are common.

- Don't judge parents who are in denial or seem to be overprotective of their child. Accept them as they are, and realize that these are common responses for parents in their situation.

- Understand that some families have had multiple experiences working with professional experts, and that their reactions to you may have nothing to do with you personally. If their experiences with other experts have been negative, it may take more time for you to build a relationship with these parents than with parents who enter the program having little or no prior experience with experts.

- Be prepared to coordinate with specialists (if any) who are working with the family. Teamwork is important in meeting any child's needs, and including specialists and family members on the team may be helpful in meeting the special needs of some children. Parents may know more about their child's condition than you do, and the specialists working with them may have expertise that you can use.

- Use "people first" terminology. Don't say "a disabled child"; say "a child with a disability." Don't say "special-needs family"; say "a family who has a child with special needs."

- Provide opportunities for both the child and the family members to integrate into the program or classroom. Introduce the family to other families, and help them to get to know each other.

- Learn about community resources that are available to all families. The family who has a child with a disability or other challenges may be able to expand your knowledge of community resources based on their experience.

- The other strategies in this book that apply to parents in general can work equally well with parents of children having special needs.

Here is a story about the benefits of parental involvement in an inclusion program.

A mother brought her baby to a "Mommy and Me" class for the first time when he was 17 months old. Her child was born with a heart defect and had had several surgeries in his young life. His main experience outside the home was with heart specialists and medical procedures. The nursery classroom was an entirely new experience for both him and his mother. His mother was shocked when she saw the skills that other children her son's age had developed. It was her first experience being around babies other than her own, and she had no idea of the developmental issues her child had been dealing with—issues that had been ignored in the interest of saving his life. She vowed from that day forward to focus more on his development and less on his medical problems, and she spoke right away to the specialists who had been seeing her son. They directed her to the resources she needed. She continued in the class, glad that he had a chance to interact with other children his age in an environment set up for play. She and everybody else was delighted at the progress the boy made in a short time, once he got in an environment that was developmentally appropriate and conducive to his needs.

Diversity of all sorts is a bonus. Everybody benefits from inclusion of children with special needs.

4 Creating an Antibias Environment

WHAT TEACHERS NEED TO KNOW

Although *antibias* is a word that some people find unnecessarily negative, it belongs to a particular tradition that those in early childhood education should know about. The term *pro-diversity* puts a positive spin on the word but doesn't connect it to the antibias movement in the same way. Many early childhood education professionals and parents first heard of the movement in the book *The Antibias Curriculum*, written by Louise Derman-Sparks and the Antibias Curriculum Task Force in 1987. This book was updated in 2010 by Louise Derman-Sparks and Julie Olsen Edwards in a new edition titled *Antibias Education for Young Children and Ourselves*.

What is an antibias environment? It is an environment without bias toward any particular group of people. It is an environment that accepts everyone. Let's start with a typical early childhood environment before the antibias movement began. You could walk into almost any classroom or child care center and look around at what was on the walls, in the dramatic play area, in the book area, and in the refrigerator. You would find pictures, books, and puzzles representing families and children of European roots. Somewhere, you'd find "community helpers" who were white and segregated by gender. The firefighters and police officers were all men, as were the doctors. The teachers, nurses, and librarians were all women. Although the food may have been reflective of local diet, it was most likely food with which European Americans in that region were most familiar. Even if the staff was diverse, the environment didn't reflect this diversity or their backgrounds. Furthermore, it was obvious that the people in charge were from one group and the aides and cleaning people were from another. This isn't ancient history. You can still find this kind of situation in some classrooms and other early childhood education programs today, although there has been some change.

Now let's take a walk through an antibias environment. Pretend that you enter the door of a classroom or child care center. You look around and see pictures on the wall representing the diversity of the children and their families—and of the greater society. You notice pictures of women in a variety of jobs and roles, as well as pictures of men in various roles. When you walk over to the book area, you see that same diversity represented not only in the pictures and stories but also in the languages. Books are available in the various home languages of the children. Some are commercial and some are homemade. In this classroom, there is a dramatic play area, which is set up for housekeeping play today; you see objects and containers of food products found in the homes of the families in the programs. A mother is sitting at one of the tables helping several children make tortillas for a snack.

At group time earlier in the week, a grandfather came in and told the whole group of children a story from his culture. Today's group time finds the children sitting on the floor with a teacher who is speaking a language other than English. She is using two persona dolls to tell a story. These are dolls the children are familiar with—they already know their names, personalities, and family histories as well as something about their cultures. The story is about something that happened between these two dolls. The story is familiar to the children, because something similar happened recently in the play yard between some of them. The teacher asks the children to help the two dolls resolve their problem, and the children contribute lots of ideas.

Part of an antibias approach is creating an environment that welcomes men as much as it welcomes women.

Creative teachers have always found ways to bring diversity into the classroom; one way is by using parents as resources. Supply catalogs once offered only a few items representing diversity. Now, of course, you can buy "people" crayons in many skin tones—whereas there used to be only one "flesh-colored" crayon in a box, and it was pale pink. Community helpers are also more diverse.

It isn't just "stuff" that makes an antibias environment. Such an environment is also affected by the attitudes and behaviors of the people in it. Organizational matters affect the environment, too. An organization with the goal of an antibias environment has a variety of people in all levels of positions and job roles—the boss isn't necessarily a European American, and the cleaning person and gardener aren't new immigrants. Antibias also shows up in the way people communicate with each other, as well as in the attitudes of respect and openness that are displayed.

WHAT TEACHERS CAN DO

- Read *Antibias Education, Second Edition* by Louise Derman Sparks and Julie Olsen Edwards.
- Analyze the environment you are in, and see if it welcomes all the people who use it. Then go into an early childhood education (ECE) environment and analyze it according to the information below.
- Does this environment reflect people who don't come into the classroom but who are in the community?
- Consider how to make any environment welcoming and reflective of all people.
- Become aware of your own behaviors that show your biases and prejudices.
- Respect all families, and don't make snap judgments about them.
- Keep a positive attitude in the face of differences.
- Give families credit for having information, experience, and understanding that may be quite different from your own. From their cultural background, history, and way of life, families accumulate what are called *funds of knowledge* that may not be recognized by teachers.
- Learn about their funds of knowledge.
- Involve families—ask them to bring in aspects of their culture.
- Pay attention to what goes on between families in the program, and consider helping them to sort out differences, like you help children. But remember, you can't be all things to all people, so if the role of facilitator for adults doesn't come easily, maybe somebody else should do it.

Here is an example of a kind of biased attitude that seems like the "right attitude" to most early childhood educators, but one that some families perceive as biased.

The story goes like this: *A teacher during her first day at her new preschool got very upset watching some of the children pretending to shoot each other. Though there were no play guns in the program, children pretended by using their fingers or any object that they came across. War was the game they were playing. The new teacher decided to do a circle time activity the next day designed to teach the children that guns are bad and war play is wrong. At staff meeting that afternoon she brought up the subject of her distress and her plan to deal with what she considered a big problem. She went on and on and even went so far as to blame parents for the gun play in the classroom. Another teacher, who grew up a military family and married a soldier, challenged her one-sided view of gun play. She suggested that this subject needed more discussion. She talked about her own children and their worries about their father, who had been overseas for a while. Her children knew he was in a war zone, that he was in danger, and that he was fighting for his country. She talked about how children play out their fears. She didn't see guns as bad—only as necessary. Another teacher who was a hunter joined the discussion and mentioned the families in the school who were also hunters. They valued their guns and taught their children to do so also. The discussion changed from a tirade to one that included different perspectives on guns. Although none of the teachers wanted toy guns in the program, they had differing ideas about how to handle the issue of children's pretend play. The point of the story is not how they resolved the issue, but how to talk out your differences and move from biased attitudes to more open ones.*

This classroom is in a rural school on the West Coast that has a number of Spanish-speaking families, mostly from Mexico.

> **SUNNY VALLEY SCHOOL NEWS**
>
> **SPECIAL EVENTS**
>
> Jason Lopez reports on the Cinco de Mayo Celebration.
>
> On May 5th we celebrated Cinco de Mayo. We had three performances, one by Mrs. Gomez's class, one by Ms. Johnson's class and one by Mr. Smith's class. Mrs. Gomez's class did a song called Rancho Grande. Ms. Johnson's class did a dance. Mr. Smith's class did a play. We learned that Cinco de Mayo is all about how the Mexicans won an important battle. At the assembly, Jerrick Palacov, our student council president gave each classroom their own flower.
>
> Jason Lopez

Taking an antibias approach means recognizing the cultures in the class.

5 Respecting All Families, Including Those with Same-Sex Parents

A book called *Making Room in the Circle: Lesbian, Gay, Bisexual and Transgender Families in Early Childhood Settings* (Lesser et al., 2005) makes it clear that early childhood educators must include all families, even ones they may not know much about. When any families are ignored, the message is strong and invites "silence, invisibility, secrecy, and shame" (Lesser, Burt, & Gelnaw, 2005).

What does it mean to ignore families? It used to be that many families were ignored because classrooms mainly reflected white people of European roots, just as the history books that teachers studied in college told only white history—and only *male* white history at that. That area of ignorance began to be addressed back in the sixties and seventies. But today, LGBT (lesbian, gay, bisexual, and transgender) families are only just beginning to be acknowledged in books and images aimed at early care and education programs and classrooms. According to Lesser, Burt, and Gelnaw (2005), "Children's identities and sense of self are inextricably tied to their families. What happens when children never hear words nor see images that describe their families? ... [T]he message is clear: 'Your family is just not something to talk about'."

One reviewer of the previous edition of this book suggested to mention in this revision that the subject of same-sex parents is about just another type of family. The issue is not about homosexuality, but rather accepting differences. When children receive unspoken messages that they are not to talk about their families, identity issues can arise. Their school lives and home lives become greatly separated. Self-esteem can be affected, which in turn can affect their ability to learn. Even though nobody says their families are unwelcome, the silence gives the message.

It's not enough to just bring in books and images, however. Early childhood educators need to understand the kinds of conditions, including political, legal, and socioeconomic ones, that affect LGBT families. Furthermore, it's important to understand "the dangers that LGBT families face: loss of children, physical violence, danger to their homes and property, unstable employment, financial insecurity and rejections from their families of origin. As educators become aware of these conditions, the ethical responsibility to provide care and safety for children takes on new meaning" (Lesser et al., 2005).

It's also important to know that there are cultural differences in LGBT families and that these may make their lives harder or easier. For example, some Native Americans believe in what are called *two-spirit people*. A two-spirit person has the gift of housing in the body both male and female spirits, which gives that person the ability to see the world from two perspectives.

The goal of your classroom or program should be to create an inclusive learning community where everyone feels safe and has a sense of belonging. One way to do this is through building partnerships. These approaches apply to programs that have LGBT families as well. In addition, consider the approaches listed below.

WHAT TEACHERS CAN DO

- Recognize that a goal for quality education and care programs is for all children to feel good about themselves. One way for teachers to support that goal is to accept a child's family even though the teacher may not approve of that family. It is imperative that children not receive negative messages about their families!

- Family-centered programs provide the best education and support for children. To be family-centered, early childhood professionals partner with all families, including LGBT families.

- Create an environment of safety and trust. Confidentiality is an important part of such an environment.

- Create a welcoming environment that invites relationship building among *all* families and between families and teachers or staff.

- Unlearn any biases you have around sexual orientation and gender identity. Oppression is oppression, and you don't want to have any part of it—either by supporting oppressive systems, practicing discrimination yourself, or harboring internal oppression.

- Learn the appropriate language related to LGBT families. Don't assume you know what anyone wants to be called; find out. The glossary in Lesser, Burt, and Gelnaw (2005, pp. 9–14) is almost sure to teach you something you didn't know.

- Recognize that LGBT parents have struggles that most other parents don't, such as asserting their right to exist as a family or keeping their family secret for the safety of their children. They also face a different set of legal issues around marriage, employment benefits, adoption, divorce, and child custody.

- Recognize that taking on challenges makes you stronger. Struggling with your own beliefs and honoring *all* families at the same time may seem overwhelming. If the struggle isn't within you, you may find it among colleagues, between them and families, or among the families themselves. It may be hard to facilitate relationships with these struggles going on, but you have to do your best.

- A simple strategy for respecting all families is to check out your forms. Do they have spaces for "mother's name" and "father's name," or do they simply indicate "parents' names"?

- Watch out for events like Mother's Day and Father's Day when not all children have connections with a mother or father. This issue doesn't just apply to LGBT families. Many children live in single-parent families with no connection to the other parent. How about skipping Mother's Day and Father's Day, and just celebrating Parents' Day?

- Address the family's strengths, not their weaknesses. Like all families, LGBT families have their unique strengths. In addition, they may have some strengths that are directly related to the challenges they face, such as the ability to express who they really are, a willingness to take risks and move toward new forms and social structures, a deep desire and commitment to being a parent, resilience, and the ability to stand up to discrimination.

Create a welcoming environment that invites relationship building among all families and between families and teachers or staff.

6 Building Partnerships

Partnerships with families are not a given in schools and other early care and education programs. Indeed, if you explore the images of the relationship between early childhood professionals and families, you may find a great variety. Expert/amateur, professional/client, and server/served are some images (perhaps unconscious) that lie in the heads of professionals. True partnerships don't fit into any of those images. Partnerships require two-way interactions and commitment. They don't come from the top down.

The partners don't have to be alike; they don't have to have the same skills. In fact, partnerships work better when the partners have different strengths—strengths that complement each other. But one thing both sides need is to have a sense of power in the relationship.

If a partnership is to exist, it is the teacher, caregiver, or director's job to initiate it. So in some ways, unless mandated, the partnership depends on the professional to make it happen. Let's examine what the professional needs to have to create and support partnerships:

1 A strong sense of a particular kind of professionalism. The usual image of a professional is a bit cold and distant. Business clothes may be part of the image. Most early childhood professionals don't fit that image, and if they are to be partners with families, they can't. They need to create relationships, and that means they can't be cold and distant. They must be warm and personable.

2 Self-respect and respect for others are two key ingredients of a professional/family partnership.

3 Clarity about the importance of building partnerships, and a commitment to doing so.

4 Sensitivity, self-reflection, and good coping skills.

Partnerships with families benefit all and serve the child better than when professionals and families work separately to provide early care and education. The family knows their child in a different way than the professional does. Family members have information about the past and present that the professional doesn't. They have visions of a future. They know the child in a greater number of settings than the professional does. The professional knows about children in general—perhaps a lot more than the family does—but not about this particular child in this family. The professional knows how this child behaves in an early childhood environment among peers and with unrelated adults when away from the family. It takes all of this information, knowledge, and experience coming together to give the best care and education to each child.

When children see that their teacher or caregiver is working together with their family, they feel more secure. The more the teacher or caregiver and the family work together, the more likely there is to be consistency between what goes on at home and what goes on in the center or at school. The child is likely to feel more comfortable when away from home if the care and education setting is in harmony with the home. The younger the child, the more important the consistency. It's hard for very young children

Partners don't have to be alike; they don't have to have the same skills. In fact, partnerships work better when the partners have different strengths.

to understand that they should behave differently in one place than they behave in another, though children do grow to have that understanding and, by the primary grades, most children understand appropriate school behaviors (even though they may not always practice them). The question is, then, is it good for every child to have to adjust to what may feel like an alien setting at first?

Professionals gain from putting effort into building partnerships by learning more about family differences and traditions. They gain anthropological information as they experience cultural differences. They can do a better job and achieve more satisfaction when they put themselves in partnership with families.

Taking a partnership approach benefits parents and other family members by giving them a greater understanding of how early childhood education works in general and in their child's program specifically. By getting involved in the program, family members gain increased knowledge of their own child in a different setting and can visualize what it is like when they aren't there. They can also carry on at home and expand on what the child is involved in at school or at the center. Parents and other family members tend to exhibit self-confidence and feel good about their child expanding his or her horizons and skills as he or she pursues new interests and projects.

There are many strategies for forming partnerships with families. In fact, every one of the strategies in this book is related to reaching the goal of partnerships. Four more are presented below.

WHAT TEACHERS CAN DO

- If you don't already have support systems, work to create some. To create partnerships with parents, you need support from the following:
  - Those above you, such as your principal, director, board, or advisory council.
  - Policies and a stated philosophy about the value of partnerships with families, and some concrete ways to support them.
  - Colleagues you can consult with and talk to.

- Find time for communication. Partnerships won't happen if you never have time to talk to parents. This strategy takes more than just a willingness. This is where advocacy comes in. You need support in the form of such things as extra staff, which is a budget issue that you alone can't solve.

- Hone your communication skills. Partnerships depend on clear communication around mutual expectations. Exchange of information is vital to partnerships. Above all, find out how to communicate with each family. Communication is more than hello and good-bye at the door, a conference or two and a regular newsletter, e-mail, or Internet blog. For one thing, not all families speak and understand English, and even those that do cannot necessarily read. If most families speak the same language—one you don't speak—consider learning it. If you have even one family that doesn't speak English, get a translator. If you have families from more than one language background, find more than one translator. Sometimes the families themselves have someone who can translate, or someone else enrolled in your program might be able to do so. Get creative! Yes, communication can be a challenge, but one well worth taking on.

- Consider instituting home visits if you don't already do them. Home visits help a good deal in creating partnerships with families, as you get to see them on their own territory. See Carol Hillman's article in Exchange (2011).

- Don't keep a one-size-fits-all image of a partnership in your head. Different families will prefer different levels of partnership. Find out from each family what level they are comfortable with. Figure out a variety of ways to involve parents. The more flexible you are, the more likely you are to get more parents participating.

When children see that their teacher or caregiver is working together with their parents or guardians, they feel more secure. With a partnership, there is likely to be more consistency between what goes on at home and what goes on in the center.

7 Removing Barriers to Partnerships

Some of the biggest barriers in communicating and working effectively with families are the attitudes of many early childhood professionals toward families, and families' attitudes toward them. Some early childhood education professionals have a bias against parents—setting themselves above the group with whom they are supposed to work. This may be an unconscious attitude, but it comes out in behaviors. It also shows up in language when professionals generalize. Conscious or unconscious stereotypes get in the way of forming partnerships with parents as well. For example, the following has been heard in staff meetings more than once—"Oh, you know how parents are," said with a sigh. That's a generalization. "Oh, those parents," said critically, can indicate a stereotypical idea that parents of a certain group don't really care about their children.

Looking into the reasons behind a negative attitude toward families, we can see a pattern that has come down through the ages. When one group feels downtrodden, lacks self-esteem, and is devalued by society, members of that group sometimes look around to see who they can regard as even lower than themselves. Because of the humble beginnings of early care and education as a field, practitioners have not garnered the esteem (such as it is) of teachers in higher levels of education. Indeed, those who work with children under five are sometimes even regarded as babysitters. One U.S. president suggested that child care could be replaced by volunteers, grandmothers, and other kindly community women so that the taxes going into public-supported child care could be saved. One huge argument against such a step is that care and education can never be separated. Another is that training makes a difference in quality. Though early childhood education professionals have nothing to be ashamed of, many of those who work with children under five still have difficulty feeling good about themselves, especially when the pay of teachers isn't as high as that of other professionals, and the average preschool teacher or child care provider, even those with bachelor's and master's degrees, keeps them at the poverty level on the economic scale.

To remove attitudes, such as those described so far, as barriers to partnerships requires changes on several levels. Early educators, as individuals and as a group, must make an effort to look at themselves differently. They must stand proud and sure. They must see themselves as professionals and discard the notion that they are a notch above "babysitters." They must work with families and professional organizations to advocate for raising salaries and status.

Above all, they must conduct themselves as professionals, which means discarding any bias they may have against parents. While professionals are trying to establish their professionalism, they may stress their funds of knowledge and ignore those of the family. They may also take on airs they consider to be professional—such as remaining cool, distant, and emotionally detached. As a profession, early care and education is still exploring what it means to be professional and retain one'sits status while building relationships with other ECE professionals and with the families and children who are served. Being too emotional and closely attached becomes a problem, but remaining distant, removed, and detached is also a problem.

Environments give strong messages. This one welcomes parents with a bulletin board full of messages and an attractively furnished meeting space set apart behind a window.

The other side of the picture is how some family members treat early childhood education professionals. One explanation may be that some family members are much higher on the socioeconomic ladder than their child's teacher or other early care and education provider, and look down on them. They are used to having power at work and may see the people who work with their children as underlings. One infant–toddler care teacher, when told she had to wear an apron, refused to do so because she did not want to suggest to the parents that she was like their maid.

Another explanation for negative attitudes of parents toward teachers and care and education providers may be that the family perceives that they are in the same boat and have the same low status. Family members may seek to rise above that level so they can look down on the early care and education staff or provider.

One possible barrier to the partnership between teacher and family relates to early experiences of the adult(s). Some family members may have had bad experiences themselves going to school as children. Just the idea of being in a classroom again may feel uncomfortable. It may not be easy to remove that barrier, but home visits might provide opportunities to build a relationship outside the classroom. That relationship may encourage the family member to try entering the classroom

WHAT TEACHERS CAN DO

- Become aware of when you are generalizing, and catch yourself. When one parent is making things difficult, it's not uncommon for the early care and education professional to complain to a colleague about parents in general. Remember, just because one parent is giving you difficulties doesn't mean that all parents are the same.

- Avoid stereotyping. Just by living in a racist and sexist society, we unconsciously take in stereotypes. The media is full of them—for example, making fun of people with accents or with differing abilities. Become aware of your own stereotypes, and move beyond them. Making an effort to get to know individuals from a group that you have a tendency to stereotype will broaden your view of them.

- When someone bothers you, do some self-reflection. Often the traits in people we don't like are traits that we have ourselves but don't see. They may not show because we are so busy suppressing them, but when they appear in others, it touches us deeply, where we are most vulnerable. This is called *projection*, and it shows up in the saying that we are more like our worst enemies than our friends.

- Be aware of how powerful roles are. The teacher who is also a parent can forget that when relating to parents in his or her program.

- Work on your own self-esteem. Take care of yourself. Stand up for yourself. Learn self-assertion skills.

- Work on your professionalism. As a member of the early childhood education profession, you are part of something bigger than yourself.

- Recognize that the body of knowledge you have or are gaining is important. Don't discount your own knowledge even though you want to be open and sensitive to parents who don't have the same knowledge.

Here's an example in story form about how strong the roles we play can be, and how they influence our behavior: *An early childhood educator, who was also a parent, went to her daughter's school for a parent–teacher conference. Though she was friends with her daughter's teacher and had talked to him a number of times, once she got into the classroom she began to feel different. She wasn't there as a friend; she was there as a parent. When she sat on the little chair on the other side of the table, she felt intimidated, even though she was aware that it was partly the furniture influencing her. When the teacher got out his grade book, her daughter's folder, and his notes, she felt stiff and uncomfortable. He seemed to feel the same. Again, she was aware that the roles they were both playing were influencing their interactions. Once the conference was over and the teacher offered her a cookie, the tone of the meeting changed. When she got up to walk out, she was herself again. She was conscious of what was happening while it was happening, but couldn't seem to lighten up the situation.*

8 Minimizing Competition with Parents

A huge barrier to a working relationship is a feeling of competition between professionals and families. Sometimes parents observe that their child behaves much better around the teacher or early care provider than around them. This can make parents feel insecure. It's important that professionals acknowledge to themselves and to parents that some of the reasons for this difference are less about skills and more about attachment. When children feel insecure and afraid, they may be scared to act out. As soon as the parent arrives, they once again feel secure and less inhibited. This feeling can result in difficult behavior. Also, the child has a closer relationship with the parent, which means that emotions can be passionate or intense. The child who exhibits only mild anger around the teacher or provider can experience a meltdown when the parent is present. It may be that the professional has skills the parents don't, but these other two reasons need to be taken into consideration.

Another factor in competition is when new or insecure teachers try to prove that they know more than family members. This can be a problem when a teacher is younger than the parents and as a result becomes defensive. As teachers and other early childhood practitioners seek to establish themselves as true professionals, they may flaunt their knowledge and power. Parents who feel insecure in their parenting competencies may look to the professional as someone who is more competent and more knowledgeable than they are.

Are these two competing for this child's attention? It looks like they might be.

A very touchy issue between parents and professionals is competition for the love of the child—whether real or only perceived. This competition can be very damaging to a relationship between the adults. It's hard sometimes for teachers, or anybody working with young children, not to compete with parents for children's affection because that affection is so rewarding. Although attachment to adults in the early care and education program is important, especially in younger children, even parents who are aware of that fact may still feel pangs of jealously if they perceive that competition exists.

WHAT TEACHERS CAN DO

- Give credit to families for their funds of knowledge. Even though the early childhood professional may be an expert on children in general, families are the experts on their own children. Both kinds of expertise need to come together if the best care and education for young children is to be provided. This may be an even bigger issue if the family's culture and yours are very different. It can also be an issue if their cultural practices differ from those you were trained in.

- Reassure the families they are number one in the child's life, and that you are well aware of that fact.

- Be aware of when you might be creating competitive situations.

- Watch out for creating excessive emotional dependence in children. Some signs include a young child always wanting to be near the teacher or clinging to him or her. Older children may show their excessive emotional dependence by making demands on the teacher's attention. Ask yourself, is it good for this child to want such a close relationship with me? When children care too much about a teacher, it can be hard on the teacher and on the parents.

- Be aware of your own emotional dependence on the children. One teacher who was absent for two days confessed that she was hurt that the children didn't miss her more than they did.

- Be sensitive to physical affection between yourself and the children. Be especially sensitive if it seems to bother a particular parent.

- Notice any "child-saving" tendencies in yourself. Become aware of any feelings of rescuing the child from the family. This is not unusual in people who work with young children in early care and education programs. Sometimes it is a stage that will pass as the person develops professionally. We can't help our feelings, but we can be honest with ourselves about them and stop ourselves from acting on them.

I remember when I was caught in the grasp of what I think of as a "savior complex." I was a new preschool teacher and was out to save many children from their parents (not all—some parents I approved of—the ones like me). Not only was I in the child-saving business, I was going to save the whole world through my work with children by raising a generation that was better than the last one. I was definitely riding on a high horse. I am glad to say I moved out of that stage once I realized that parents play a much more important role in children's lives than I ever would, and that I needed to team up with them, not look down on them.

9 Supporting Attachment

∙∙

WHAT TEACHERS NEED TO KNOW

Although issues around attachment to teachers and other early care and education practitioners can create difficulties in parent–professional relationships, attachment is important for all children. The younger the child, the more attachment comes into the picture in early care and education programs. This chapter is focused on the reason for and appropriate approaches to take related to attachment when working with children under three years of age. Think of this chapter as explaining preventive measures to take against attachment disorders. Attachment disorders impede development, get in the way of relationships and make learning harder. The point of this chapter is to explain what helps children who are in out-of-home care early in life arrive in preschool, kindergarten, or primary grades unimpaired in their ability to feel secure and relate to others and to progress in their development and learning. It's not that an infant–toddler program alone can prevent attachment disorders that may be occurring at home, but it can go a long way toward helping keep the damage down. That's why creating a relationship with one or a few special people is vital in infant–toddler programs. Even if children have a firm and close attachment at home, they still need a relationship that is personal, steady, and ongoing if they spend more than a few hours each time away from the family. Feelings of trust and a sense of security come from appropriate attachment and allow the child to develop and learn.

Research being done on the human brain points to the importance of attachment and caring relationships in the first years of life. Bruce Perry (2006), in his lectures and writings, talks about the chemicals that wash over the brain and cause damage when babies experience continual abuse and neglect or live in unusually stressful environments. Without attachment, babies suffer. With a firm, healthy attachment, the baby has a better chance of getting through the hard times with less damage (Perry, 2006). The Pikler Institute, a residential nursery for infants and toddlers in Budapest, Hungary, is based on the concept that attachment to caregivers is a vital ingredient of the first years of life, and that it allows even institutionalized babies to grow up to be whole, healthy, and fully functioning adults. David and Appell (2001), Gonzalez-Mena (2004), Petrie and Owen (2005), and Shonkoff and Phillips (2000) have made a strong case for caring relationships. When babies feel secure in a healthy attachment, their brains are able to develop without harmful chemicals interfering with the process. Studies of resilient children indicate that even one close and caring relationship can make a difference even in the face of continual hardship (Werner, 1995).

Attachment to a caregiver, teacher, or provider is a concern for many families. "Will my children still love me if they spend all that time away from me while I'm working?" is an agonizing question many parents ask themselves. Teachers and caregivers should be reassuring if they perceive that a parent has this concern.

When families watch their children get attached to someone outside the family, they may have conflicting feelings. For some, it is a relief that their child feels comfortable and safe away from home, but mixed with that can come feelings of being replaced. Some families feel competition for the child's affection. When caregivers and teachers seem to know more, have better skills, and can handle their children better than the families can, the feelings of competition can be devastating.

Attachment is important for all children. The younger the child, the more attachment comes into the picture in early care and education programs.

Being a teacher, caregiver, or provider is very different from being a parent, though children should be attached to both. The following are some of the differences:

- The child's attachment to the family is and should be closer than the attachment to the professionals.
- The child has both a history and a future with the family. The relationship of the early childhood professional is more short-term, with the exception of some family child care providers who may work with the same child for 11 or 12 years, and with the family for even longer if there are siblings. But even then, the future of the child is still in the hands of the family, not in those of the professional.
- The length of the relationship of the child to the early childhood professional is less predictable. Children can leave the program at any time if the family changes programs or moves away from the school.

As children grow older, if they have a firm sense of themselves and feel secure in their attachments at home, most don't need such a close, one-on-one relationship with an adult in out-of-home programs. Kindergarten and primary teachers have a larger group size and ratio of children to adults, so the amount of one-on-one personal attention drops compared to that in prekindergarten and infant–toddler programs. Skilled teachers who understand the value of these relationships can still form healthy attachments even in these situations so that all children feel valued and close to their teacher.

WHAT TEACHERS CAN DO

- Take attachment seriously. If you work in an infant–toddler program, and policies to promote attachment aren't already in place, do what you can to create them. That may not be easy because such policies are often dictated by the structure of the program. In that case, advocacy becomes vital. Policies to promote attachment in children under three should include:
  - **Small group size**—The younger the children, the smaller the group needs to be. Starting with infants, a good group size is six infants with two caregivers.

This way the caregivers can get to know a reasonable number of children, as well as their families (Lally, 1995). As children get older, the group size can increase. In some states, 20 is considered a reasonable group size for K-3.

- **Primary caregivers**—Especially for children under age three, each professional should have several children for whom he or she is primarily responsible and works to become attached to. This is not an exclusive relationship, and there should be other caregivers who also know the children individually and as a group (Lally, 1995). By kindergarten, especially if children have learned to be functioning members of a peer group, one teacher will work, though it is desirable to have several adults, including some parent volunteers, in the classroom. That way children get more individualized attention from adults. Family participation is another benefit.
- **Continuity of care**—This is a concept that applies more to infants and toddlers and, to some extent, preschoolers than to those in K-3, though some schools use what's called a *looping system*. Continuity of care, or *looping*, means keeping children together for longer periods rather than promoting them to a new room and teacher. In some programs, infants and toddlers are moved (or promoted) on a regular basis each time they reach a new stage of development or have a birthday instead of their staying together as a group with the same teacher. Keeping the group together with the teacher means that as infants and toddlers outgrow the environment, the environment either needs to change or the group and teachers need to move together to a new room. For infants and toddlers, two or three years gives them and their parents a chance to become attached to the professionals.

- Communicate with the family about the policies and their purpose. Explain clearly that attachment to the early childhood professional is not meant to compete with attachment to the family. The family attachment should always be closer because it is far more important and long-lasting than any other attachment.
- Support the child's attachment to family. Some ways to do this are to have pictures of family members available at the children's eye level. One program encourages family members to bring an article of clothing that has the smell of a close family member on it for the baby to sleep with.
- Acknowledge the child's feelings for the family members to whom he or she is most attached. Assure those family members that they are number one in the child's life. Another way to support the child's attachment to family is to honor diversity in your classroom, no matter what age you work with.
- Be aware that some families may feel threatened by seeing evidence that their children care about their teachers, and do what you can to help these families feel more secure. Watch out for the following pitfalls:
  - Encouraging lots of physical affection from children, especially if you see the parent looking uncomfortable when the child comes back for yet another hug and kiss.
  - Letting a child call you mommy or daddy. Correct them if they do. Let parents help you decide by what name you should be called.
  - Taking pride in being the first to see a child reach a milestone. "Your baby took his first step today" can be a devastating announcement to parents who wished they could be there to see it. Let the parent make the discovery that the baby is starting to walk and announce it to you.
- Look inside yourself and explore your own feelings about a particular child or family. It's natural for professionals to have strong feelings about a child or group of children. Some professionals go through a "savior stage" of wanting to rescue children from their parents. Acknowledge your feelings, and at the same time become fully aware of your actions. You can *accept* the feelings without *acting on* them.
- Understand that professionals establishing attachment should focus on optimal distance, while promoting optimal closeness in family attachment.

10 Considering Authority

One issue that sometimes comes up between early childhood education professionals and families is the question of who is the authority in what situation, and how does that authority behave. In school, when a parent is there and the child breaks a rule, should the parent step back and let the teacher handle it, or should the parent take care of it? At an open house at school when children come with their parents, if the children are out of order whose job is it to correct them? Or, at a child care center when the staff and parents put on a party for newcomers to get acquainted, the children are invited, and a group of them gets too wild, whose job is it to settle them down? In a family child care home, when a child starts jumping on the couch, is it the parent's place to stop the child (even if jumping on the couch is allowed at the child's home), or is it the provider's job?

Sometimes this is not a problem. One party or the other may step forward and manage the behavior appropriately, and both may be in agreement about what is the right thing to do. At other times, both parties wait for the other to do something, resulting in out-of-bounds behavior of the child, lack of guidance, broken rules, and maybe even damaged property. Such situations can also result in a sense of confusion or insecurity on the part of children, who know they are out of bounds and expect someone to do something about it. Alternatively, if one adult steps back and the other steps in because the other isn't doing anything, that action may result in hurt feelings or resentment on the part of one or both adults.

An additional issue having to do with authority comes when the teacher sounds and acts very different from what the children are used to. In that case, they may not see the teacher as an authority. This issue brings up the subject of cultural and economic diversity. For example, a well-trained teacher may have an approach to guiding children's behavior that is very different from what a particular child or group of children experiences at home. The soft, unemotional tone of voice the teacher uses in a guidance situation may be a tremendous contrast to the stern voice and manner of the family member in charge of the children at home. Children who are used to strict, sharp, no-nonsense guidance may completely ignore what the teacher is saying. The following is an example.

An energetic, active boy who is new in the class keeps getting in trouble. The teacher just doesn't know what to do. He doesn't even hear her when she talks to him in the sweet, honey-flavored voice she is used to using with the children. She is quite concerned about this "problem child" and calls a conference with his mother. The two of them arrive and instead of sitting down beside his mother he starts running around the room knocking things off of shelves and creating chaos. The teacher says to him, "I want you to sit down now, dear." He ignores her. She issues her request several more times with the same result. The mother looks at her in amazement. Finally the teacher looks at him intently and says, "if you don't sit down, you won't get a star on your star chart." He laughs. His mother rises up in her chair. She says his name loudly and sternly while looking him in the eye. He stops and looks at her. Then she points her finger at him and then at the chair. He walks over and sits down obediently.

Who is the authority in this situation if a child misbehaves?
WHWH

WHAT TEACHERS CAN DO

- Find out more about how your guidance approaches fit or don't fit with what the children individually and as a group are used to. What works well with one child or group of children may not work at all with another.
- Study cultural differences in how authorities behave by observing, asking families, asking other teachers, and reading.
- Understand yourself as a cultural being. Become aware of how your training as a teacher does or does not fit your culture.
- In the case of misbehavior when both teacher and family member are present, determine who will be the authority in each setting or situation. Who has the primary responsibility for the child's behavior? This is not something you can look up in a book—it has to be decided among the parties involved.
- Plan ahead so there is agreement as to who is in charge.
- When a situation occurs where the authority issues haven't been settled, discuss the situation out in the open.
- Anticipate situations and discuss them ahead of time. For example, at a parent meeting, one preschool center discussed the expectations they had for parents to be in charge of their own children at an upcoming party with family members and staff. The families agreed that it would be up to them, even though the party was taking place in the center, where the teachers usually provided guidance for the children.

11 Focusing on Family Strengths

WHAT TEACHERS NEED TO KNOW

When a family you are trying to build a partnership with is struggling with many challenges, you try to empathize with them. You seek to understand what it is like to walk in their shoes. Perhaps, at the same time, you think about the ways you can help them, and also consider the resources the community has to offer. All these approaches are valid, but they also lead you to focus on the family's problems instead of its strengths. Turnbull and Turnbull (2001) said, "Highlighting and appreciating families' strengths is one of the key aspects of supporting families to enhance their own self-efficacy" (p. 67).

A key to working with all families is to be sensitive, understanding, empathetic, and remember their strengths. You're not a therapist, but you can be an ally. Just by listening and talking you can show your support. By having faith that people can use their own abilities to succeed in life in spite of obstacles, you can help them heal. Think about people in your own life who have believed in your strengths and recognized your potential.

When you think of strengths, think also of cultural diversity. How much do you understand the various cultures of the people you are working with? Without understanding, you may fail to see strength in factors you might consider a weakness. You don't have to take a course in anthropology to be open to learning about other cultures. You're also bound to learn more about your own as you begin to perceive differences.

It may be hard to shift focus from problems to strengths, but think about the approaches described below that you can take to make such a shift.

"Highlighting and appreciating families' strengths is one of the key aspects of supporting families to enhance their own self-efficacy"
(Turnbull & Turnbull, 2001, p. 67).

WHAT TEACHERS CAN DO

- Look at how you are defining the family. Can you see how they are unique and special instead of downtrodden and miserable? Are you aware of the skills, strengths, and special talents that each member has? Think about their resources.

- If you don't know enough about the family to see its strengths, do you have ways to find out? Having conversations with family members is one way. You may not have much time to talk to families, but if you are dedicated to partnerships with parents, you know that conversations are essential if you are to get to know and appreciate each family.

- Storytelling is another way to learn about family strengths. When we hear each other's stories, it makes us remember our own. Stories can be healing. As you listen to stories, remember to think in terms of possibilities instead of dwelling on problems.

- The challenges that individuals and families face do not necessarily weaken them. Sometimes these challenges give them the strength and courage to grow, develop, and move forward. Don't assume that challenges always result in damage.

Perhaps the child who drew this picture comes from a family that has a love of music as one of its strengths.

- Help the family keep their focus on their dreams and aspirations instead of on what is happening right now. Help them concentrate on a life without the challenges they face at the moment. If they can visualize that life, they can aim for it.
- You may have expertise, but the real experts in this family are the members themselves. Help them tune in to the expertise they have.
- Help the family members empower themselves by making them aware of the choices they have.
- You may have resources to offer, but help the family members tune in to their own resources and focus on their strengths, skills, and potentials.
- Focus on protective factors rather than on risk factors. For example, a family that has a broad base of support for the parents, and is a member of a community, has an important protective factor to stand up against the risk factor of ill health or a financial crisis.

What are some strengths that families show even when they have big problems? Here are some examples of strengths families can have—either as a group or as individuals within the family:

1 Strong attachment that shows up as love for their children, and which is reciprocated.

2 An extended family network that they can rely on.

3 The ability to speak two languages plus one dialect.

4 Good social skills.

5 Persistence and stubbornness. They don't give up.

6 Physical strength, body awareness, and good health habits.

7 A strong sense of humor.

8 A love of making music and listening to it.

9 A cheerful outlook.

10 A variety of interests.

11 "Street smarts." They know how to get along and keep safe.

12 Mutual support.

13 A knowledge of how to "work the system."

12 Helping Parents to Be Advocates for Their Children

WHAT TEACHERS NEED TO KNOW

A role for family members that comes naturally to some, but not all, is to advocate for their own child. For those family members who don't see themselves in this role, it's up to the teacher or other early childhood professional to help them understand that they have a right to be their child's advocate.

How does a family show that they are advocating for their own child? When a parent comes to the teacher with concerns about her child, she is being an advocate. If a parent sees the teacher at the end of the day and asks how the day went, he is usually asking about his own child, not as much about the teacher's day. It's not that he doesn't care about the teacher or want to know about the rest of the class; he mostly wants information that relates to his own child. When parents and other family members focus on their own children, they are being advocates for them.

When family members stand up for their own children in the face of all the others, their attitude may put them in opposition to the professionals whose role is to advocate for the group rather than singling out one child in that group. For example, a family who doesn't celebrate any holidays asks for a meeting with the second-grade teacher whose curriculum is built around holidays and seasons. The teacher may think, "Why doesn't it seem unreasonable to this family member that the other children be denied their pleasure for the sake of a single child?" When the teacher understands that families are advocates for their own children, then the request or demand makes sense. Another example in a preschool occurred when one family member who comes from a culture where women stay covered up complained about her four-year-old daughter running around without a shirt on, which was common practice in the program on warm days. Still another family member who came from a state where there are hookworms in the soil complained about his child running around barefoot and wanted the child's shoes left on at all times. Neither request is unreasonable. Yet both requests make it hard on the teacher—first, to remember the individual requests, and then, to carry them out when most of the other children are shirtless and shoeless. It becomes even harder when the two children concerned want to join the crowd and do what the rest of the children are doing.

Although it may seem wrong to make exceptions or to change a whole program for one child, think about the idea of including children with special needs in a classroom set up for typically developing children. Individualizing can be as important for *all* children and families as it is for those with special needs. Parents or other family members can help the teacher individualize by advocating for their children with special needs. They can also help other parents or family members advocate for their children if they arrive in the school already experienced in advocating for their own child. It's sometimes the case that by the time a child leaves infancy the family has already had lots of practice in advocating.

It's important, when thinking about families as advocates for their children, to be fully aware that being a parent is very different from being a teacher. Keeping this fact in mind is vital to working well with families. One difference, according to Lilian Katz, is that families are particularistic—they favor their own children over others, have an emotional stake in their children's welfare, are biased in favor of their own children, and put the needs of their own children first, even at the expense of other children's needs. Early childhood education professionals must be universalistic—concerned about every child in the class or group without bias, not put any one child first at the expense of the others, and apply skills and resources to each child.

WHAT TEACHERS CAN DO

- Appreciate when parents stand up for their own child. This is a healthy kind of bias, even though it may make your job more difficult. All children need an advocate who takes their side.
- Support families in their role as an advocate for their child.
- Help families who don't have strong advocacy tendencies to acquire them. Part of this approach involves asking them about their child on an ongoing basis. You can also introduce them to families who do have advocacy tendencies.
- At the very beginning of your relationship with the family, ask what their goals are for their child. Better yet, ask what their *dreams* are for their child. Erma Bombeck, a humorous author, wrote, "It takes a lot of courage to show your dreams to someone else." That's why forming a relationship and building trust with families is so important! Asking parents about their dreams for their children is an approach that Jean Monroe, national early childhood consultant and trainer based in California, suggests. Parents who discuss their dreams rather than their goals for their child tend to set their sights higher. After you ask, really listen to what they have to say. Make it a point to always listen to them when they talk about their child.
- See the families' natural tendency toward advocacy as something that can be expanded to advocacy for the program in the face of budget cuts, for example.
- When the family's advocacy tendencies conflict with your perspective, practice holding their perspective in mind as well as your own. It's a matter of becoming self-aware—observing yourself from a distance even when engaged in an emotional conversation. Keep reminding yourself that it's good they are advocating for their child.
- Be flexible. Acknowledge that there are whole realms of possibilities in addition to the ways you are comfortable with or have always done things.
- Learn win-win negotiation skills.
- Keep in mind the differences in roles between parent and professional. Your relationship with the child is short term and can end abruptly. You don't have a history or a long-term future. You're not the parent.

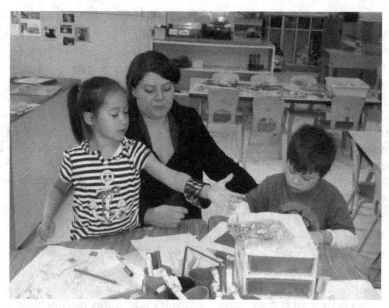

Parents who participate in early care and education programs tend to be advocates for their own children, and some go on to become advocates for children in general.

Encouraging Parents to Become Advocates for All Children

13

When looking at partnerships, families who advocate for the program stand out! Some of these families started out by advocating for their own child and then ended up becoming advocates for the group of children of which their child is a member. A natural progression for some families is to focus on their own child first, and then later on the class or group their child is in. Some move beyond that to advocating for the entire school or program. Other families skip all those steps and become advocates for children in general.

The importance of child advocacy is a lesson that many who enter the field of early care and education learn, whether they are professionals or parents. Children can't speak for themselves, so adults have to speak for them. When budget cuts come to school districts or child care programs, who can speak for the children? When school districts or state departments of education mandate a curriculum that is developmentally inappropriate, culturally inappropriate, or harmful in other ways, who can speak for children? The voices most heard are those of parents—the consumers. Some families are natural advocates and understand the process. They will protest on their own, without urging, when their children can't get what they need from the powers that be. Other families have to learn to be advocates. They can learn a good deal from those who teach in or run the schools or other early childhood education programs their children attend.

Advocacy can start close to home and may feel uncomfortable for the professionals at first when they are a target, such as when the families are advocating for the teacher or program to change. One example was reported by Jim Greenman (reported in Gonzalez-Mena, 2008a). A group of African American parents got together and told their teachers that they didn't want their children to go outside anymore. The teachers started a parent education campaign to make sure the parents understood the influence of gross motor development on cognition, and the importance of fresh air and exercise to health. They continued with the outdoor program, but the parents continued demanding a change. It wasn't until the two sides finally sat down together and the teachers asked the parents what was behind their demand that the true problem came out into the open. It was the sandbox. Children were coming home with sand in their hair, which was causing all kinds of problems, including rashes, ringworm on the scalp, even damage to the hair. When the two groups put their heads together and started brainstorming solutions, they came up with one—shower caps for children who play in the sandbox.

Though this particular situation put families and professionals on opposite sides at first, they eventually ended up on the same side, with everybody focusing on what was best for the children. Even when the ending isn't so satisfying, the fact that parents

Some parents and other family members start out by advocating for their own children and then connect with other families to advocate for the group of children of which their child is a member.

mobilize themselves must be seen in a positive light. When parents find energy as a group to push for change, that energy can be used again when an issue comes up facing the program. If the funds are cut and the program is in jeopardy, it's possible that the families will team up with the teachers and advocate to save it.

What can families advocate for? Certainly, saving their own program is one thing; saving schools in general is another. A bigger advocacy project is changing the lives of children in poverty. If all children are to succeed in school, the factors working against that success need to be eliminated. Poverty is a huge factor! Marion Wright Edelman (2011) who founded the Children's Defense Fund, saw where advocacy was needed and did something. She took on leadership in more than one movement to improve the lives of children in poverty, starting back in 1964 when the Mississippi Freedom Schools came into being during the summer of 1964. Today as head of the Children's Defense Fund (CDF) she and her staff keep track of what's going on in children's lives, and report in regular updates of *The State of America's Children*. The latest report shows that the picture of children in poverty is not good! Poverty hurts all children, and especially children of color, who also face bias and discrimination. With poverty comes poor nutrition, hunger, and health problems, all of which get in the way of children's ability to develop, learn, and take advantage of education. As an industrialized country, the United States makes a very poor showing in comparison to the children of other industrialized countries. Advocacy can make a difference, and the CDF is constantly advocating. What are some approaches to helping parents along the road to advocacy for all children?

WHAT TEACHERS CAN DO

- Realize that families organizing and advocating can be beneficial even though you may disagree with the target of their advocacy efforts. Keep in mind how effectively that energy can be used when you are all on the same side.

- Help families see the big picture. Advocating for children involves speaking out for giving all children access to high-quality, developmentally and culturally appropriate early childhood educational experiences in rich, safe environments. There is great inequality in schools, and that needs to change. Programs for children under five may not have well-trained or well-paid teachers. That needs to change as well. Child advocates have made progress and will continue to do so, especially if their numbers continue to grow with the addition of families who are served by schools and other early care and education programs.

- Encourage advocacy even when the need isn't evident, and teach parents how to be effective advocates. Recognize all the places that advocacy works, such as school boards and other governing bodies, regulatory agencies, and lawmakers at the community, state, and even the national level. Early childhood education has benefited greatly in the past from family advocacy efforts.

- If families don't organize themselves, help them. Recognize potential leaders among families, and nurture their leadership qualities. Start by brushing up on your own leadership skills. Debra Sullivan's 2010 book *Learning to Lead* has many useful ideas.

- Help families understand the many courses of advocacy action. The following are just a few suggestions:
  - Create or join an advocacy group
  - Collect information about a critical issue
  - Find and share research that relates to the issue, and formulate a position statement
  - Form or join a legislative telephone or e-mail tree
  - Keep up with the issue in the media, and write letters to the editor
  - Understand how laws are made
  - Develop a relationship with lawmakers, and keep in touch with them about the issues that concern children and families

Here is an example showing how one person can make a difference. Read on to see what one town did to respond to child abuse in their community (Gonzalez-Mena, 2009): When a baby died as the result of abuse, a group of residents, led by one individual, decided to do something. This was in the time when child abuse was just beginning to be recognized as widespread and a threat to children's mental and physical health. Though laws were in place at the time, the laws were not enough for this particular group of citizens, who wanted to prevent abuse in their community, not just punish it. This motivation on their part coincided with some funding set aside for prevention, intervention, and treatment of child abuse. The group went to work.

First, they established a hotline for parents to call, just to talk, when they felt as though they might not be able to control themselves. Then, they began to educate the community about child abuse and about using the hotline. This group soon discovered that what parents needed was a variety of support services. Some needed parenting information and skills, some needed respite child care, some needed a job, some needed a place to live, and some just needed relief from the many stresses in their lives that led them to take out their frustrations on their children. The picture was much bigger than anyone had ever suspected.

Today, many of these services are in place, including parent support and education groups, respite child care, an emergency aid fund, part-time temporary home services with a helper coming into the home to assist with household chores, child management, and other services. In addition, there is an innovative service called "phone friend" for children who come home from school to an empty house. All this because one person cared and figured out how to involve others in advocacy.

14 Creating a Sense of Community

WHAT TEACHERS NEED TO KNOW

Partnering with families is an important goal for teachers and other professionals in early care and education programs. A related goal is building a community of the partners. Think of a community as a group of people connected by some common interest or purpose. By that definition, a classroom or early care and education program can certainly become a community. Sometimes it happens naturally, but usually it takes a little effort to facilitate the making of those connections. It doesn't have to be hard. Think of how a good hostess moves among guests, introducing them to each other and making a group of individuals or couples into a party. Some of the skills of a good hostess apply directly to the goal of forming children, families, and staff into a community. The purpose is different of course, because the main objective is not just social but rather an enhancement of the children's educational experience. Also, the focus is longer than a party—not just for an evening but for perhaps a year or even more. Sometimes the connections families make with each other in early care and education programs last for a lifetime!

In 1980, Ethel Seiderman cofounded an organization called the Parent Services Project as a way to support families. The idea was to focus on families instead of just on children. In a book about the Parent Services Project, called *Stronger Together*, Lisa Lee (2004) explains the benefits of community building. "One of the gifts of family-centered programs is the creation of caring communities. Connected to one another by their children, adults in such places care about and help one another...Families use the center as a place to connect with one another. When good things happen for one family, everyone celebrates. When problems occur, people are concerned and work together... [I]n such a place, children grow up feeling safe, covered in a quilt of warmth from the adults in their lives."

So how do early childhood professionals turn a group of people into a community? Seiderman is a master at turning groups into communities. She did it for a number of years, starting before the Parent Services Project, when she was a child care director and ran a family-centered child care program. Her idea was to support the parents in supporting the child. That idea is blossoming in schools and other early childhood education programs across the United States, partly because of Seiderman's long-time commitment to changing the focus from the child to the family, and from the family by itself to the community as a whole. Seiderman says that the Parent Services Project emphasizes the idea that parenting is not just a private concern of the family but a community-wide concern. One way to broaden the parenting role is to give teachers and parents new ways of supporting each other.

Marion Cowee, a preschool director for many years, explains how to create a community from a group of families. "You have to make sure that everybody has a sense of belonging." Cowee doesn't mean just the parents—she suggests "finding out who are the potential members of this community. Include everyone who is important in each child's life, including grandparents, aunts, and nannies." She makes clear that the goal is to help everyone feel they belong in your classroom or program. Marion and long-time toddler and preschool teacher Lynne Doherty, who has taught in early childhood programs for many years, contributed to the following list of strategies.

Your attitude makes a difference. If you are trying to build a sense of belonging, you will invite family members in regularly. One way is by having an open-door policy that encourages family members to drop in whenever they want. Some teachers have a strong reaction to that idea, however, and consider it too disruptive. Kitty Ritz, a first-grade teacher, has solved that problem. Twice a week, she sets aside a half hour at the beginning of the day for family reading time in her classroom. This is one of the many ways that she gets to know the parents and they get to know each other. That's another secret to minimizing disruptions when family members come to visit— get them involved in productive ways that don't disturb the children. Make them part of the children's routine.

The following are additional ways to create a sense of belonging and make the kinds of connections that turn a group into a community.

WHAT TEACHERS CAN DO

- Create a sense of belonging from the beginning by finding out what everybody with whom you come in contact wants to be called. Then, work on learning all the names—including the correct pronunciation. This is not an easy job if the program or class is large, but it is a good way for early childhood professionals to work on their own learning skills as models for the children.

- Introduce everyone who is part of the program or a support to the classroom, such as aides, cooks, custodians, and bus drivers.

- Help people get acquainted by putting up a picture board of the staff, with a little something written about each person. It could be a short biography, or a statement of what the person likes about working with children and families, or a list of hobbies. Put this where families that drop off their children can easily see it. Some programs include substitutes on the picture board as well as regular employees.

- Consider a picture board of families as well, with a few facts or statements about each one. Put this up where staff and other families can see it.

- If the entry area has the space, consider not just a bulletin board planned and maintained by the staff, but also a bulletin board for parents that they plan, maintain, and interact with. An interactive idea to put on the family bulletin board is a changing survey, with space for family members to write under a question. For example, a question could be "What is your child's favorite restaurant?" This kind of question gives parents something to talk to each other about.

- In a preschool setting, if children arrive with a family member each day, have the room set up for a free play period, and make yourself available to greet children and adults. When children enter an interesting environment, they can separate more easily and also become engaged with the materials and with each other. That gives adults a chance to talk to each other briefly, both at the beginning of the session and at the end.

- Introduce families to each other. Note where personal connections are forming, and later on, suggest that maybe the family consider changing the emergency form to include new friends, rather than the distant aunt in another town whom the child barely knows, to come get the child when necessary.

- Help parents become resources for each other. Carpooling is one way they can work together and gain a sense of belonging to a community.

- Use the intake interview, if there is one, to begin getting acquainted, including finding out what special interests or skills family members have.

- Make sure your environment is welcoming to everybody. Check to see that it reflects an antibias point of view—one that includes everybody in the classroom and community beyond. A welcoming environment means that images on the walls include everybody, the languages of the families are represented, and adaptations are made for people with disabilities—both children and adults. One program wanted to make sure that all the books they had available for the children gave welcoming messages, so they taped a clean sheet of paper to the inside cover of each book with the suggestion for parents to write their comments and reactions to the book. It soon became clear that what one parent loved, another felt offended by. In this way, both parents and staff learned about differing perspectives about what feels welcoming.

- Having an address list is a good idea so that families can connect with each other on their own. Be sure you have permission from each family to put their name and contact information on the list.

- Fund-raising is a way for family members to get to know each other by working together. Be careful to recognize that some families have children in more than one class or program. Fund-raising can get to be a burden in a large family.

- Always think of meetings as a way for people to get to know each other, no matter what the purpose of the meeting is. Start with an icebreaker to loosen people up and get them relaxed and interacting.

- This entire book is full of ideas about how to make families and staff into a community. In particular, look at Strategy 28 for ideas about how to set up the environment for communication, Strategy 22 for ideas about how to get families to participate in the program, and Strategy 6 for ideas about how to build partnerships with families.

A picture board of the families in the program helps to create a welcoming spirit and a feeling of belonging.

15 Understanding and Appreciating Cultural Differences

· ·

WHAT TEACHERS NEED TO KNOW

What is *culture* anyway? "Culture is a shared system of meaning, which includes values, beliefs, and assumptions expressed in daily interactions of individuals within a group through a definite pattern of language, behavior, customs, attitudes, and practices" (Maschinot, 2008, p. 2). A worthy goal is for teachers and other early care and education specialists to become culturally sensitive and begin looking for the meaning of parenting behaviors and beliefs they run across in the families they serve. Though it may seem as if a step toward that goal is to examine lists of cultural traits of various groups, that approach doesn't work. Those lists are generalizations, and generalizations can promote stereotypes.

Understanding cultural differences has to do with recognizing yourself as a cultural being and coming to understand that the way you see the world, organize your behavior, and look at children are, to a great extent, influenced by your own culture, which also may have been influenced by your training. It's hard for teachers and other early care and education professionals (including family child care providers) to know what to do when parenting practices raise questions, yet the professional is trying to be culturally sensitive and responsive and to build a good relationship with the parent. How does this professional honor and respect diversity when parenting practices don't fit personal and professional definitions of best practices? How can teachers and providers respect and honor practices that seem to be incomprehensible, bad, wrong, or maybe even harmful?

If you haven't thought about diversity in terms of contradictions, this idea of honoring what seems wrong may confuse or upset you—even put you off balance. Those feelings are not bad—they can serve you well, because when we enter a state of disequilibrium, that's the perfect condition in which to learn something new. If we suspend judgment, we can come to understand that what looks wrong from our personal perspective may look right to someone else. We can learn something by looking through someone else's eyes. It's uncomfortable to begin questioning what we already know, but it's important to do so when working in an early childhood setting that includes diverse families that you don't see eye to eye with.

Of course, causing harm to children is not something we can tolerate, but when we really begin to understand another's perspective, we may see how something that seems to hurt children doesn't when regarded in a different context. Instead of just taking the behaviors at face value, our job is to look beneath them to see if we can discover patterns of meaning.

A saying from Dianna Ballesteros, a child care director who is a long-time advocate for the antibias movement in California, clarifies this point. Dianna says, "En cada cabeza hay un mundo"—"In each head there is a world." Expanding the world in one's own head is the means to understanding people who are different from one's self, and it goes far beyond just celebrating differences in ethnic foods, music, and customs. By acknowledging that each person has a different reality, you take the first step toward beginning to understand it.

What about the diversity involving child-rearing practices that a teacher considers wrong? Take, for example, a family who sends a baby bottle in the lunch box of a kindergartener for snack time. As the teacher gets to know the mother, she realizes that the family is "babying" this child in more ways than one. In the teacher's language, "babying" has negative connotations. The mother and older siblings do everything for the child, which means she is often passive and seldom tries to do anything for herself, including putting on her own coat. When the kindergarten teacher talks to the preschool teacher, who has the same family in her program, the kindergarten teacher discovers that the mother is still spoon-feeding the four-year-old at home, even though both children feed themselves fine when no one is there to help them. The teachers worry to each other about these children's sense of independence—their self-esteem and their competence to take care of themselves. They agree that developing self-help skills is a major task of the early years. "Babying children" like this family is doing harms the children's sense of themselves as individuals!

These teachers are engaged in dualistic thinking, which makes it seem that if their ideas are right the family has to be wrong. They want to be culturally responsive to the family, but they can't condone what the mother is doing. The teachers are coming from the context of Western culture and perspective, and they have the support of others who have the same kind of background, education, training, and experience. From their view, this family's practice is known to cause harm. They even know the term for the type of harm—it's called *overdependence*, or even *codependence*, and it results in the need for counseling when children grow up.

From another perspective, neither of these practices is harmful—indeed, these practices are just the opposite. They are not only beneficial but also necessary in view of a particular set of goals. In his 1981 book, *Beyond Culture*, Edward Hall, an anthropologist, uses an old saying about "apron strings" to explain differences. He writes, "The world can be divided into those cultures that prepare their children to be independent individuals and live apart from their family of origin as adults and those that do not. Those cultures that do not emphasize independence and individuality prepare their children to remain closely tied to the family as adults, living in close proximity if not in the same house, dwelling, or compound." In other words, one group cuts the apron strings, and the other does not.

For many people trained in early care and education, it is easy to see why cultures cut the apron strings, and how they raise their children in preparation for this cutting. For those people, it may be hard see the other view, and they may be extremely resistant to it.

Families who don't cut the apron strings see independence and individuality as a threat, not a goal. They are confident that their children will grow up to be independent, but they worry that they will be *too* independent and leave the family behind in their quest for individuality. So starting at birth, the caregivers in these families dampen the flames of independence when they arise, and instead teach the value of being dependent and of having others dependent on you.

One way to look at these differences is to regard them as two different patterns of meaning. Names given to these particular patterns vary, but calling the teacher's perspective *individualistic* and the families' perspective *interdependent* is one way to label them (Maschinot, 2008). The families who cut apron strings teach children self-help skills and encourage them to acknowledge the feat. "I did it all by myself" is not considered bragging but as an example of being proud of one's individual accomplishments. Children are encouraged to make individual choices and think for themselves. They are taught to be assertive. The families who aim at keeping bonds strong and families together downplay skills showing independence, which they figure are naturally built in and will arise no matter what. Instead of helping children take pride in individual accomplishments, they teach a skill that some would call "graciously accepting help." Children in interdependent families are taught that close connections and collaboration are more important than personal self-development. Lessons in being self-controlled, conforming, and cooperative are important in interdependent families. Respect for elders and putting your needs and desires aside for those of others are also important lessons that children learn in these families—quite a contrast to the individualistic cultures.

People are usually so immersed in their culture that they don't think of why they are doing what they are doing, only that it feels right. If asked, the parent stressing interdependence might say that they *like* doing things for their children, or maybe that their children are too young to do things for themselves. They might not be able to explain that they are trying to keep their children close to them and create strong, lifelong ties. Most people have a hard time explaining their culture or how their actions and attitudes relate to it.

WHAT TEACHERS CAN DO

- When something about a family's practices really bothers you, try to look at what they are doing through their eyes instead of your own.
- Recognize that income level affects culture and can be a factor in a family's practices.
- Stay open and put aside judgment long enough to gain a deeper understanding than first impressions allow.
- Accept differences even if you don't perceive a cultural reason behind them. It may be easier for you to accept differences if you think that people have a valid cultural reason. Consider people of your own culture who think differently from the way you do. Their reality is just as valid as the reality of someone who has an entirely different culture as a backup. Just because a family that is doing something we disagree with is of the same culture as us doesn't mean that they don't have their own reasons for their practice. Work as hard to understand them as you would to understand families of cultures different from your own.
- Keep in mind that doing things for children doesn't necessarily make them grow up helpless and forever dependent. The modeling process is very strong. Children imitate what they see others doing. If one grows up seeing people helping others, they too become helpers, in addition to receivers of help. Putting that modeling effect together with a lifetime of lessons in respect for elders, you can see that it might result in the younger persons helping the elders when the time comes that the elders need help.

Here is an example from my own life about how I learned to see a cultural difference in child rearing practices. Teresa, who was from Mexico and a staff member in a program where I once worked, helped me see a perspective on meeting needs that was different from my own on the subject. I was telling her how important I thought it was for children to learn to meet their own needs as soon as possible. My argument usually went like this: If we meet our own needs, we are more able to help those who can't meet their needs. The flight attendants say in the plane, "In case of a loss of cabin pressure, put on your own oxygen mask before helping others." Behind that statement is the idea that if you lose consciousness, you won't be of any use to anybody else. Well, that's the way I was looking at the issue of meeting needs—we have to look out for ourselves first. And I've never forgotten what Teresa said in response: "Janet, that's so sad. If you are looking out for yourself, that's only one person concerned about you.

But if instead of focusing on yourself you think first of others, and if everybody else does the same, that's lots and lots of people looking out for you." That conversation stuck with me. It gave me a new way to think about things. I was able to see her point and honor our differences, but I didn't shift my whole frame of reference to become a person who no longer values independence and individuality. I am still who I am. I still have a particular set of values that relate to the way I was raised, my family of origin, and my culture, which I label as European American, white, Anglo, or Celtic American, depending on to whom I am talking. I am who I am, but I now have a broader perspective on differences.

Celebrate all families!

16 Establishing Culturally Responsive Education and Care

WHAT TEACHERS NEED TO KNOW

Why culturally responsive care and education? Children are adaptable; can't they just learn new ways of doing things? Besides, doesn't it make sense to aim to create bicultural people? Shouldn't that be a goal of education? What if parents, both immigrants and nonimmigrants, want their children to learn what they consider the "American way" and don't want their practices at home and/or their home language to be part of the school or program? These are all questions that come up in discussions of culturally responsive care and education.

Let's start with the last one first. It's true that parents may make a big separation between what goes on at home and what goes on at school or in early care and education programs. For example, at university lab schools, the foreign students who enroll their children often express a desire for their children to learn English and experience "American culture." They know their family will return to their own country, and they see the potential for their young children to go back home bilingual and with an understanding of a culture different from their own. They don't see a risk of their children losing their language or becoming alienated from their own culture.

That's a different situation from an immigrant family who has chosen to come to this country, for whatever reason, or a refugee family who ended up here but never chose to come, or a family who has been on this continent for many generations but came involuntarily, or an indigenous family that has been here for countless generations. Each of these families may have widely differing ideas about what they want for their children and what part their home language and culture should play in their child's education and development.

Imagine two families coming into a program. One has recently fled from a country where they enjoyed high socioeconomic status, and both parents are well educated. Though they are now poor, they have a different set of hopes and expectations from the second family, who arrived three generations ago, have made their living as migrant farm workers, and have children who still speak their home language. There is no way to generalize about the hopes and dreams these families have for their children without asking them. But the answers to the questions in the first paragraph may be pertinent to the separate situations described in this paragraph.

The answers to the rest of those questions fall into several themes. One is identity formation. Another is keeping connections to families strong.

The younger the child, the more unformed is his or her identity. The questions to be answered in terms of identity formation are who am I and where do I belong. According to J. Ronald Lally (1995), "Culture is the fundamental building block of identity. Through cultural learning, children gain a feeling of belonging, a sense of personal history, and security in knowing who they are and where they come from. The school or child care experience should be in harmony with the culture of the home" (p. 66). Lally wants teachers and other early childhood professionals to pay great attention to incorporating home practices into educational and care settings.

A story illustrates the identity issue: A girl named Ana entered kindergarten and proudly wrote her name for the teacher on the first day. The teacher said, "No, that's wrong; *Anna* has two n's," and the teacher corrected her spelling. Ana went home and told her mother that her name was spelled wrong. Her mother was adamant that the teacher was the one who was wrong. Ana was forced to choose between her mother and her teacher. She chose her teacher. Thirty years later, when Ana told this story, it was with tears running down her cheeks. She said the simple thing that happened in kindergarten affected the way she felt about herself, her family, and her culture. At the age of 15, she decided to reclaim her identity, but just talking about it brought more tears. Such a little thing, but such big repercussions!

Here's an example of where the teacher's goals have an effect on the child's behavior at home: A third-grade teacher is trying to get children to think for themselves. She feels the basis of a democratic society is for children to learn to question authority. To that end, she sometimes makes mistakes on purpose to see if the children will correct her. At home, however, a child in her class is taught respect for her elders, and the teacher's goals are in direct contrast to her family's. This child did fine at first, until she began bringing school behavior home. She began to question older family members, which caused a good deal of dissension in the family. Then, she began to disagree with them. The whole household was disrupted by this new behavior.

With younger children, such a basic practice as feeding can be an issue. In a particular child care program, children are encouraged to practice self-help skills from early on. That means that when babies are old enough to eat finger food, they are given the chance to do so. One parent in the center has a strong reaction to arriving one day and seeing her child fingering pasta in tomato sauce and making a big mess. In this family, no one ever touches food with their fingers—even sandwiches are eaten with a knife and fork. The lessons in acceptable behavior that their baby receives at the center are diametrically opposed to what the family teaches at home. Phillips and Cooper (1992) said, "Feeding has patterns of meaning that are shared by and embodied in the lifestyles of a larger group" (p. 11). So instead of explaining the importance of early self-help skills to this family, a better approach would be for the caregiver to try to understand the patterns of meaning behind their approaches to eating. The teachers and caregivers in these examples need to discuss the differences in practices with family members and discuss with each other whether the programs should become more culturally responsive and, if so, how to do that. Such discussions might not be easy.

WHAT TEACHERS CAN DO

- To start thinking about how to create culturally relevant classrooms and programs, listen to what parents want for their children. Go beyond their first statements. Discuss with them the deeper aspects of their dreams and desires for their children. Ask about what the parents know about other people's experiences. Discuss biculturalism and bilingualism. Although the information about diversity at the beginning of this chapter is important, you can't automatically understand a family by putting them in some broad category, such as "immigrant." You have to get to know them.

- Learn more about identity formation. Become aware of what messages you are sending to individual children about what is appropriate and inappropriate.

Think about how your messages are influencing each child's sense of self, sense of cultural competence, and feelings of belonging.

- Reflect on your own early years and identity formation. How did you gain a sense of self and learn what culture you belonged to, and how well did you fit in with your family? Do you have some leftover feelings about what happened to you? Identity formation is a subject that some teachers, caregivers, and providers have never thought about before. Knowing yourself can help you better understand others.

- Think about your own educational experiences and how well they did or didn't fit with your home culture. Are you a person who grew up in a family that spoke a language other than English? Did you retain the family language or lose it when you learned English. How do you feel about that?

- If someone came into your classroom or program and looked at the environment, what culture or cultures would they see reflected there. Could they tell anything about the diversity of the families of the children who spend time in that room?

Working with Conflicts Around Education and Care Practices

17

....

WHAT TEACHERS NEED TO KNOW

Dealing with conflicts around education and care practices is a huge subject and weaves itself throughout many of the strategies in this text. Because it is impossible in a small space—or even in a lifetime—to condense all differences that can occur, this particular strategy focuses on a set of contrasting patterns that influence how people see children, determine what they need, and develop educational and care practices to fit their perception and approaches.

Bridging Cultures in Early Care and Education (Zepeda, Gonzalez-Mena, Rothstein-Fisch, & Trumbull, 2006) explains two organizing concepts, or patterns, which the authors call *individualism* and *collectivism*. This particular framework is just one way in which to explore cultural and individual family differences when conflicts arise. In research done on elementary schools (Rothstein-Fisch, 2003; Trumbull, Diaz-Meza, Hasan, & Rothstein-Fisch, 2001), these concepts have been shown to be accessible and highly useful in improving home–school understanding.

When early childhood education professionals view family priorities and value systems in a nonjudgmental way, they learn not only about other cultures but about their own culture as well. Culture passes from one generation to another through child-rearing practices. Culture is mostly invisible, except when it bumps up against differences in other values and belief systems through interactions. The two basic concepts— *individualism* and *collectivism*—help make visible how culture influences a person's attitudes, beliefs, values, and behaviors. Each orientation is associated with a different set of priorities that often shows up in care and education practices.

What are the differences between these two patterns? People with a strong individualistic perspective see the importance of children learning that they are unique and special individuals, so these adults stress independence and individual achievement. The focus is on the needs of the individual, self-expression, and personal choice. Physical, emotional, and mental exploration in a safe environment is often a priority. Objects become important as sources of learning about the world and how it works. Adults teach respect for personal possessions.

Although taking the individualistic perspective may seem "normal" or "natural" to you, most of the world's cultures (70% according to Triandis, 1989) and many families in North America have more collectivistic tendencies and place a higher priority on interdependence than on independence. People with a collectivistic perspective are more likely to emphasize group needs over individual needs. Social responsibility is important to people with a collectivistic orientation. They also tend to stress respect for authority and group norms. Personal possessions are downplayed, and human relationships are more important than objects.

WHAT TEACHERS CAN DO

- Remember that the concepts of individualism and collectivism are merely tools and can't be considered more than that. Don't use these tools to oversimplify or categorize people and families. It's important to refrain from stereotyping people or putting them in cultural boxes.

- Also remember that all conflicts over child-rearing differences are not cultural ones. Some may result from a family tradition, an individual experience, specific kinds of training, and philosophical ideals.

- In the face of differing ideas about early care and education practices, seek to establish common ground with individual families and groups of families without simply imposing regulations, rules, and restrictions.

- Look around to see if the program is highly individualistic. The physical environment is likely to reflect this perspective, with children having their own desks, cubbies, lockers, or coat hooks identified as "theirs" and with their names and pictures prominently displayed. Children are encouraged to take care of their property, take care of themselves (e.g., do their own work, take care of toileting, and feed and dress themselves), and use "their words" to identify their wants and needs. All of these examples are signs that individualism is valued.

- Look for the parts of the program that may reflect a more collectivistic orientation, which stresses respect for authority and obligation to group norms. In collectivistic settings, possessions are often shared, with objects being important in the context of human relationships, and not in and of themselves. For instance, children may not be urged to play with objects or to investigate them independently. In a more collectivistic setting, there is more emphasis on the group than on the individual. The collectivistic perspective favors large groups for activities over small-group or individual activities, and also mixed-aged groups where older children help younger children.

- If you find yourself to be more on the individualistic side, consider whether your emphasis on having children "do their own work" might be modified sometimes to having children work together with partners or in groups.

- If you use competition to motivate children, consider how this might affect children who come from more collectivistic families where competition is frowned upon.

- If you like to give special attention to individual children to reward them for something outstanding that they have done, consider that for some families taking an individual out of the group and putting him or her in the limelight brings up uncomfortable feelings.

- Become a student of cultural differences and remember that the more you learn about diversity the better able you are to develop an appreciation for these contrasting patterns of care and education, and understand that they need not be mutually exclusive.

- See if you can use these two organizing concepts—individualism and collectivism—to figure out how to remain sensitive to each family's needs and wants even when they conflict with your own ideas or the program's practices.

Sometimes it looks as though people with a more collectivistic orientation "baby" people. Here is a short story about a woman who enjoyed "babying":

Roz was a family child care provider who emigrated from Taiwan to the United States as a child. Once, in a meeting of early care and education professionals, someone said it was important not to do anything for children that children could do for themselves. Roz looked skeptical and quickly said that she disagreed with that statement. She then talked about how her grandmother loved to "baby" her, even after she grew up. Roz felt it was very important that she let her grandmother take care of her, because it made the old woman happy. It didn't matter that Roz could do for herself what her grandmother did for her. Roz's response started a lively conversation as various people gave their opinions about independence and interdependence.

Jan, another family child care provider, spoke up with passion in her voice. She said that she always hated to be "babied" when she was a child—and that she hated it even more so as an adult. She said that she felt resentment toward people who didn't let her do things by herself.

Like most people, Roz and Jan don't call themselves collectivists or individualists; nevertheless, these two have very different viewpoints about being helped or helping themselves. If someone were to observe them working with children and families, it is likely that their two perspectives would have a visible influence on their behavior.

Putting a priority on self-help skills may indicate a more individualistic orientation, which may be uncomfortable for some families with young children.

18

Considering Cultural Differences in Guidance and Discipline

. . . .

WHAT TEACHERS NEED TO KNOW

In some classrooms and other early care and education programs, issues can arise when the behaviors of the teacher or other adult in charge don't mirror the kinds of behaviors the child is used to at home. Images of authority are important when it comes to child guidance For example, if the teacher takes a too-soft approach, using gentle words and a neutral tone of voice when correcting children, some children may ignore this teacher. If they are used to a very different tone of voice, children probably won't think that the teacher means what she says. If the teacher doesn't follow up and persist, these children may disregard rules and limits and perhaps become labeled as "problems." In some cases, the real problem is that the children misinterpret the meaning of what the teacher is saying. For example, some children are used to the way that the adults in their families and extended kinship networks assert their authority at home and in the neighborhood, which might include stern voices, meaningful facial expressions, and strong body language, which are followed by immediate action if the words and "the look" don't work. For example, Lonnie Snowden (1984; Gonzalez-Mena, 2008a) says, "The Black community invests effective responsibility for control of children's behavior in an extensive network of adults.... Because of this extended parenting, children's behavior receives proper monitoring and more immediate sanctions than is the norm in American society. Children may be expected to develop more active exploratory tendencies and assertive styles, since respected external agencies can be counted on to reliably check excess" (p. 135).

This approach is a contrast to teachers who expect children to develop inner controls or self-regulation. The idea is for the individual child to incorporate what is appropriate and what is allowable, sometimes called "the rules," and use inner controls to guide his or her own behavior. That's very different from knowing that any adult around will correct misbehavior.

Reward systems may not be familiar to some children and may seem strange. Reward systems include praise, star charts, and ways of earning special privileges for good behavior. Some children react negatively to the manipulative aspects of such systems. Some families may be uncomfortable with such systems as well—especially when they don't work or they produce side effects.

When authority figures behave in ways that aren't familiar, children can feel confused (Phillips, 1995). Furthermore, some children are used to firm, strict, and sometimes even physical guidance, and without it they keep testing the limits. They may even come to the conclusion that the teacher doesn't care what they do. These children can end up labeled as "problem children" (Hale-Benson, 1986).

It's important to note that firm limits actually give some children more freedom because they know that somebody will stop them if they go too far. When the teacher just talks and doesn't stop misbehavior, they continue to push to find out what the limits are. Children don't recognize that they are getting guidance and direction from the adults in that situation, but that those adults aren't like the ones at home. Instead of being strict and insisting on certain behaviors, these adults are stressing individual choice. The lessons then come from the children living with the consequences of their actions. The adults don't scold or threaten. They don't punish. They allow natural consequences; that is, for example, the child experiences what it's like to be cold when he refuses to put his jacket on to go outside. The consequences must be reasonable ones—ones that don't harm the child but that may feel uncomfortable. When there are no natural consequences, they set up the situation so that there are logical consequences (Dreikurs, 1990). An example of a logical consequence comes when an adult is reading a story and the children aren't paying attention. The adult closes the book and says, "Well, if you won't listen; I won't read." The adult can do this in a matter-of-fact manner, without even changing facial expression or tone of voice. It's not meant as a punishment, only as a consequence of the children's own behavior.

Cynthia Ballenger (1992) writes about the problem of children's confusion over adults' authority when Haitian children encounter teachers who stress individual choice and living with the consequences of that choice. Their Haitian teachers didn't think in terms of individual choice, but rather they defined behavior as either good or bad. They warned children that bad behavior would bring shame on the family. They told the children that they had a responsibility to be good, and scolded them when they weren't good. The teachers regarded reprimands as ways to strengthen the relationship and show children that someone cared about them and their behavior. That is a contrast to more neutral approaches that avoid reprimands, allow children to make choices to discover what the consequences are, and put responsibility on the individual. For some people the consequences approach seems cold and cruel. For others it seems a good way for children to learn.

Then there is the issue of time-out. When spanking became questioned by many experts and some families as well, using time-out seemed an acceptable alternative. Some people use time-out as a substitute for punishment. Some make it sound like punishment just by the words they use and by the tone of their voice. Others see time-out as meeting a need in children who are over-stimulated and not able to control themselves. But in cultures or groups where shunning is the worst possible punishment, time-out is not considered acceptable for young children.

I learned firsthand about the difference of feelings around using time-out with children when I was leading a workshop in the Southwest: *A number of cultures were represented in this workshop, including some Native Americans. The subject of time-out came up. Immediately the group split and arguments emerged from both sides. The people who brought up the subject thought everyone would agree that time-out was a good way to handle misbehavior. But the other side had strong arguments against using time-out. A group of people announced that time-out was forbidden in their centers. When asked why, one said that in prison the worst punishment is isolation! Why would we do to children what the worst criminals suffer. Another said a misbehaving child needs the group, not separation from it. Another pointed out that in some communities the worst offenders are shunned by the group—shut out. No child can possibly misbehave in a way that should bring the worst possible punishment down on him or her. It's just much too strong a punishment for any offense a child could commit.*

So how do you work with parents around cultural differences in guidance and discipline? Are you aware of how much of what you learned in your training about guidance and discipline fits your own culture?

WHAT TEACHERS CAN DO

- When the teacher acts one way and the family another, it calls for serious discussion to find out the family's perspective and to share yours. It's not about right and wrong, but about differences (that is, unless child abuse, as defined by the law, is part of the situation). If you already have a relationship with the parent and there is mutual trust, it will be easier to talk about how to help the child get along both at school and at home.

- Start by observing the parent with the child, and suspend judgment if the parent's behavior doesn't match the way you approach guidance and discipline.

- Have the parent observe how you handle misbehavior, and talk about it afterward.

- If there is a drastic difference, expect the dilemma to be resolved eventually, but probably not right away. Try to learn about the parent's approach, the reasons behind it, and the expected outcomes. If this is a cross-cultural situation, you may both have something to learn about the other person's cultural values.

- Explain your approach and why you do what you do, but don't try to sell it to the parent. This should be a mutual exchange of information.

- Continue to work on the relationship.

- Try different approaches with the child if the ones you use don't work and the ones the parents use do. That doesn't mean you have to give up your own values or imitate the parent. By all means, don't do anything you perceive as harmful to the child.

- Open your mind to the idea that what you view as harmful may not be so in the context of the family or their culture. For example, if you are trained in the principles of early childhood education, you won't use name-calling as a way to guide behavior because, in general, such a practice is regarded as detrimental to children's self-image. But if parents call children a name, or use some kind of label, you can't know and shouldn't judge what that name or label means to the child, especially if it is a cross-cultural situation and in a language you don't speak.

We don't know if this teacher's style matches the style of the child's parents, but she does look like she means business, even if she is being gentle about it.

19 Working with Families Around What You Believe Are Harmful Practices

WHAT TEACHERS NEED TO KNOW

A difficult situation arises when the early childhood professional finds out that what the family is doing is harmful to the child. If abuse or neglect is suspected, the professional must report it to the authorities. A behavior or practice that doesn't fit the legal definition of abuse is a different matter. This is a delicate situation and must be handled sensitively. If you confront the family member with accusations, you may destroy the relationship that you have been building. If you ignore the situation, the child may suffer.

Take the example of a first-grade teacher whose student says that her mother spanked her that morning on her legs. This teacher feels strongly that spanking is harmful, but there are no bruises or even red marks on the child's legs. The teacher knows that spanking is legal as long as there are no lasting marks. She is concerned about this child and this family, but as she gets to know them better, she discovers that spanking is the only method they know for guiding their children. If the teacher managed to talk them out of using spanking as a disciplinary measure without giving them some other ideas of strategies that make sense to them, the family would be left without any way to guide their children's behavior. That would be a grave disservice to the family. So instead, the teacher started a series of discussion groups on discipline, which were very popular and widely attended. All the parents who came, including the mother who concerned the teacher, seemed to get a great deal out of the sessions.

Here's another example of a potentially harmful practice. A grandmother enrolls her three-month-old granddaughter in your infant center and tells you that she is to be put to sleep on her stomach. When you hesitate, she insists that the baby can't sleep on her back. Besides, it's dangerous, she says, because the baby may spit up and choke. You think the grandmother is just old-fashioned or uninformed. But then she plays the cultural card and tells you that it is a tradition in her culture for babies to sleep on their stomachs. Should you be culturally responsive and go along with her, or will you argue that babies sleeping on their stomachs are at risk for SIDS (Sudden Infant Death Syndrome)?

It will help both the baby and your relationship with the family if you seek to understand more about the grandmother's ideas and cultural traditions. It's important to recognize

54

that in some cultures SIDS is less of a risk than in others, especially if babies never sleep alone. Co-sleeping is common practice among many families. Also, regardless of culture, certain medical conditions put babies in more danger when on their backs. That is not to say that you should automatically go along with what the grandmother says. You would be professionally remiss if you didn't share at least your understanding of the research that indicates babies are at greater risk for SIDS when sleeping on their stomachs. Statistics may not impress her, but try to state things in terms she might listen to. Don't argue with her. Share your information in an open way, and ask her more about her point of view. It might help to find out if this is a common belief in her culture, or if some members of her culture (or even her own family) have a different view of stomach sleeping. After all, it wasn't even a generation ago that everybody in the United States who followed medical advice placed babies on their stomachs to sleep because it was considered safer than back sleeping.

A cultural practice that may startle teachers, caregivers, and providers is something called "coining," a healing or preventive practice of some people in various Asian cultures, which involves putting a special liquid on the skin and then rubbing a coin or a spoon on the area. The rubbing is hard enough to leave lasting red marks and, unless you understand it, may appear to be an abusive practice.

One person's approved healing or preventive practice may seem abusive to someone who doesn't understand it. For example, think of immunization. If people had no idea about immunization, what would they think of a parent letting someone stick a needle in his baby's arm? The parent might explain to the doubters that this is a preventive measure and that it doesn't harm the baby. But the observers might not believe it, especially if the baby cried in pain at the shot—and especially if she got sick later on. Unless the observers were from a culture that believed in science and could accept the technical explanation of the procedure, they would have to take on faith that this was indeed a preventive measure, because they saw with their own eyes that it hurt the baby and made her ill. What would it take for someone who knew nothing about Western science or medicine to understand? What would it take for you to understand a healing or protection practice that was contradictory to Western science or medicine? We all need to be open to the idea that our way isn't the only right way.

WHAT TEACHERS CAN DO

- Don't judge immediately. Seek to understand more. Barbara Rogoff (2003) suggests that even though judgments may be necessary, we can make better decisions when judging if we can move beyond the idea that our ideas are the only right ones. Only when we can see a situation in context and understand perspectives, ideas, and beliefs other than our own can we make wise judgments.

- At the same time that you are making sure not to judge too quickly, don't hesitate to report abuse when it meets the legal definition of your state. Too often children die while the people who could have saved them held off reporting suspected abuse.

- You may also be constrained by policies, regulations, standards, or licensing when you consider what to do about something that seems to be a harmful practice. That doesn't mean that you shouldn't try to understand it, but you must also consider the restraints on you.

- In all events, try to preserve whatever relationship you have managed to build with the family.

- Work on your listening skills. Using imagination helps, too, as you try to see things from a perspective not your own. Try what Betty Jones and Renatta Cooper (2006) call "the believing game." They say, "Imagining another person's perspective on things requires the suspension of reality (what I really believe) in order to pretend. (This is what someone else believes. Could I, if I tried hard?) In the diverse world we live in, we keep encountering people who don't believe what we believe. We can sneer at them, or fight them, or pretend they're invisible (until they step on our toe). Or we can accept the challenge to 'embrace contraries'" (p. 23).

- Find people from diverse backgrounds with whom you can have discussions. Then, ask questions, and learn more.

20 Thinking About Differing Ideas Related to How Children Learn

WHAT TEACHERS NEED TO KNOW

Family members remember their own education when they judge the classroom or program their child is in. Those who were taught to sit up straight at a desk, may be critical of a classroom with tables and chairs and maybe a reading corner that has cushions on the floor. If, on the other hand, they enjoyed an early educational experience like the historic Summerhill School, where play was part of the curriculum and children made decisions about what they wanted to do and where they wanted to do it (indoors or outside), parents may frown at their children having to sit at desks in order to learn.

Readiness issues can be on many family members' minds when they enter early childhood programs. Obviously, families want their children to do well in school, so they may want a strong push for academics in kindergarten and first grade, beyond what research shows is developmentally appropriate (Copple and Bredekamp, 2009).

Family members' ideas about what should happen before kindergarten can vary greatly even in the same family. Early childhood educators who work with children under five may also have varied opinions about this subject, but those who have been trained in early childhood principles and practices are likely to have a developmental view. They probably see play as part of the curriculum, a view that not all parents share. Thus, conflicts can arise. It's not unusual for a family or a group of families to push the preschool teacher for early academics, hoping that their children will be reading before kindergarten. When professionals argue the perspective of developmental appropriateness, they may convince some families, but others will dig in harder, pushing their point of view.

Sometimes the family's ideas come from messages they hear that are based on misinterpretations of brain development research. The pressure for early academics is strong from all sides.

Sometimes ideas about teaching academics arise from cultural differences rather than misunderstandings about brain research. Here is an example: A Chinese mother's own experience in learning to read in her native language influenced her ideas about how children should learn to read in English, even though learning characters takes different skills than learning to read in a language that uses an alphabet. She thought her child should be sitting down and memorizing words instead of playing with play dough and finger paint at preschool. Instead of arguing with this mother, the child's teacher listened to what she had to say, even if the teacher didn't agree with her about

Although some people think that learning is all in the head, others know that body movements are also important for learning. This scene isn't considered recess, but is part of the educational program.

what was best for the child at this stage of development. Staying away from arguing created more of a partnership atmosphere, and the mother and teacher eventually became collaborators instead of adversaries.

One prerequisite for entering a dialogue is for early childhood education professionals to explore their own attitudes toward particular parents or parents in general. They should do some soul searching about what they truly believe, and explore emotional hotspots that can get in the way of good listening. It is also useful if they can become articulate about the program's policy on readiness so that they can explain it to parents who have a different idea, without coming on too strong or arguing. If professionals believe in the policy, they can put aside their defensiveness and learn about a different perspective from their own. Thus, the people in question can create a useful dialogue. Once they have heard each other enough so that they have a bigger picture than originally, maybe they can stop taking sides and begin to figure out what is best for the child or group of children in the setting.

This is one of the many situations where good listening skills are necessary. Professionals need to make sure families feel that they are heard. They also need to work hard to understand just what it is that families want. If after some dialoguing there is still disagreement, conflict resolution or consensus building skills are needed. Be sure that any process toward resolution builds the relationship instead of tearing it down.

Getting children excited about learning is a goal common to most early childhood programs. Sharing that goal with parents can be useful. The joy of learning comes when children are encouraged to become creative, competent explorers and problem solvers. Play and exploration may not look like educational activities to some parents, but when they understand that their children are learning how to learn, they may come to appreciate the approach as useful.

WHAT TEACHERS CAN DO

- It might be worthwhile to start by examining your personal philosophy about how children learn. Write a list or a statement of what you believe and know about the learning process in children. Then you can decide if you agree or disagree with the ideas about learning stated below. When you are clear about what you believe, it may be easier to listen to and understand ideas that contrast with yours.

- Regard the environment as an important learning tool, especially when such an environment reflects and validates diversity.

- Consider a child's exploratory tendencies as an important learning skill. In the preschool years, and even in kindergarten and the primary grades, those tendencies lead children down the path to learning. Teachers of the K–3 level can provide for exploration by using manipulative materials in math lessons, for example. Exploration may look more physical than mental, especially in very young children, yet those same qualities are what inventors, discoverers, and creators throughout history have used to add to the body of knowledge that exists today. How many explorers go straight to their goal? Not many. Amazing things are discovered while meandering.

- Value dramatic play and encourage young children to pretend. Some interesting research based on Vygotsky's work has been done by Bodrova and Leong (2007) on a program called "Tools of the Mind." Hone your observation skills, and help parents hone theirs so that the value they put on play is increased when they observe what their children are learning as they play. Parents may even come to see the benefits of allowing free play for longer periods (rather than regarding it as recess—a time to rest from learning). When adults understand how capable most children are of rich, creative play, they may interrupt it less and step back so that they don't direct it or take over.

- Model resourcefulness yourself so that children see you as a learner. When children ask why, work with them to find the answer. Furthermore, let parents know what you are doing, and invite them to be part of the process.

- Help parents see how they can use encouragement rather than praise so that children are more likely to regard learning as its own reward and depend less on adult recognition of success. Help parents understand the benefits of emphasizing intrinsic rewards that come from the inside by saying, "You must feel so good about what you just accomplished there." Extrinsic rewards are rewards from the outside and make children dependent on somebody else for motivation to learn. Extrinsic rewards can be social rewards—praise or something tangible, like a piece of candy. Use these kinds of devices, even star charts, sparingly, and don't set up competitions to see who gets the most rewards.

- Don't argue about any of the preceding suggestions. Become aware of the difference between an argument and a dialogue. The purpose of a dialogue is to understand—not to win. The idea is to expand one's knowledge rather than trying to persuade the other person to accept a different point of view.

- Instead of arguing, offer families opportunities to observe you with their children, and then model what you believe in. The idea is not to win the family over but rather to expand their views—just as your goal should be to expand your own views through observation of families interacting with their children, as well as ongoing dialogue with the family.

- When creating a dialogue, remember that communication involves listening as well as talking. Sometimes we have to listen twice as much as we talk if we are to gain a bigger picture and a deeper understanding.

*Families have differing ideas about how children learn—some think
they should be active, and others think they should sit at desks and
concentrate on seat work. Even the room arrangement can be a point
of contention. Every family might not agree about this classroom setup.*

21 Managing Conflicts

Though the long-term goal of conflict management is to resolve the disagreement, the immediate and ongoing goal should be to keep from destroying the relationship while trying to reach consensus. The key to both goals is effective communication. Communication is a huge subject and has its own section, as well as being woven throughout this book. This particular strategy is aimed at seeing how to take two seemingly opposite points of view and figure out what to do that will work for everybody. An approach taken by Isaura Barrera (Barrera & Corso, 2003), a professor of special education at the University of New Mexico, involves what she calls *third space*.

Third space has to do with moving from dualistic thinking to holistic thinking in the face of what seems to be a contradiction or a paradox. If a family member whose child has been in a preschool where children learn mostly through play arrives in kindergarten to see children sitting at desks doing seat work, it's possible that she and the teacher have very different concepts about what children need in their early years. On the other hand, the teacher may be doing what she has to do rather than what she wants to do. For this discussion, let's say this teacher believes that seat work is an important way that children learn, and that play is not.

Here's another example from an infant–toddler program. Say a family member starts toilet training her baby at six months of age and the policy of the center is to wait until after the second birthday. This can create a conflict.

In these examples, both parties have reasons for what they are doing. The teacher in the first and caregiver in the second may think "I'm right, and she's wrong." The family members in both examples may think the opposite of the teacher and caregiver.

If arguments start, it's likely that the school or the center will win if the parent perceives the power to be in their hands—especially if policy, regulations, research, or experts are quoted, which can tip the balance in favor of the school or center. However, family members who lose arguments probably won't feel like partners with their child's teacher or caregiver.

Aiming for third-space solutions means that conflicts move beyond winning and losing, relationships flourish, and nobody has to give in. The idea of everybody winning in the face of a conflict flies in the face of logic for many Western thinkers, who are used to competitive situations in which there is always a loser.

Another factor that can get in the way of reaching a third-space solution is what could be called a *blind spot*. The problem with blind spots is that we don't know we have them. As I once said to a friend who has tunnel vision, "So is it like looking through two paper towel tubes and everything else is black?" He laughed and said to me, "Janet, what I don't see out of the corners of my eyes is exactly like what you don't see out of the back of your head!" My friend has a blind spot and so do I, but I never think about it.

What does tunnel vision have to do with this conflict over play versus seat work or toilet training? Let's say that the teacher thinks seat work is very important for children's success in school. She has the principal's support and district policy to back her up. When faced with a parent who wants play in the classroom, she may feel she's right and the parent's wrong. In the caregiver's case, let's say that the caregiver has knowledge and experience when it comes to toilet training and has had a hand in setting the program's policy. She is confident in her approach. When faced with a family member whose ideas clash with her expertise and program policy, she judges the family member to be wrong, because she has a blind spot that she is unaware of. She is missing a whole piece of what toilet training means to this family, just as the teacher in the first example doesn't know what play means to that family. Both professionals consider the families' approaches to be a *problem*.

If told the conflict should end in a win-win solution, both of these professionals would feel stuck in the face of a paradox. How can they solve this problem? To be culturally or individually sensitive, do they have to give in to something they believe is unrealistic, wrong, or even harmful?

No! Barbara Rogoff (2003) says, "Understanding different cultural practices does not require determining which one way is 'right' (which does not mean that all ways are fine). With an understanding of what is done in different circumstances, we can be open to possibilities that do not necessarily exclude each other" (p. 14). Often when faced with a dilemma, the teacher who is trying hard to be culturally responsive may just give in when he begins to see a cultural view that's different from his own. But you don't have to give up your own ways when you learn about cultural differences. Instead, put assumptions aside, and seek to understand rather than judge. You can make some guesses as to what cultural patterns are represented in such a situation, but you may not be right. Rogoff recommends that you continually test and revise your ideas. As she reminds us, *"There's always more to learn"* (p. 14).

It is possible that the teacher and family members are closer in their ideas than they think. If they didn't put themselves on opposite sides, they might be surprised at what they could come up with. In the toilet training example, the family's ideas likely are related to cultural or family traditions and have patterns of meaning that the caregiver doesn't understand. (See Strategy 17 for examples of differing patterns of meaning.) On the other hand, the family may have picked up on a new idea that isn't part of their tradition—but something a friend told them about . One family got excited about a new idea called elimination communication and figured they could save a lot of money on diapers. They couldn't depend on family tradition to help them learn this method, but they found a website (www.diaperfreebaby.org) that explained it. They learned how to partner with the baby by paying close attention to his elimination patterns and signals so they could hold him over a potty – just like the other family for whom this was a centuries' old tradition. Will it make a difference to the caregiver whether the particular toileting practice is a cultural tradition or a new idea? Let's hope not. Knowing that there are reasons for what the parents are doing that are valid in their minds, however, may still not bring comfort to the caregiver when facing the paradox of two seemingly incompatible approaches.

Parker Palmer (1997) gives advice about how to look at the positive side of paradox. He writes: "We split paradoxes so reflexively that we do not understand the price we pay for our habit. The poles of a paradox are like the poles of a battery: hold them together, and they generate the energy of life; pull them apart, and the current stops flowing. When we separate any of the profound paired truths of our lives, both poles become lifeless as well. Dissecting a living paradox has the same impact on our intellectual, emotional, and spiritual well-being as the decision to breathe in without ever breathing out would have on our physical health" (p. 64).

"Paired truths" is a useful term when working to see a paradox as positive, but that concept may be difficult to understand when the people in conflict see themselves as on opposite sides. They still have to figure out what to do.

Barrera and Corso (2003) give some insight into how to use third space in this situation. "A third-space perspective does not 'solve the problem.' Rather it changes the arena

The first step in working toward consensus when conflict surfaces is to suspend judgment and try to understand the other person's perspective.

within which that problem is addressed by increasing the probability of respectful, responsive, and reciprocal interactions. In so doing, an optimal response to the situation becomes more likely" (p. 81).

One way to enter that area is to move from dualistic thinking to holistic thinking. In dualistic thinking, contrasting ideas are looked at as dichotomous, which gets in the way of trying to solve problems. If it's right, it can't be wrong. If it's bad, it can't be good. If it's blue, it can't be yellow. When you move from dualistic thinking into holistic thinking, you don't separate differences into opposites. An example of holistic thinking is to bring blue and yellow together to make green. Blue keeps its blueness and yellow keeps its yellowness, and together, they make something new altogether. Green is an example of third space.

Bredekamp and Copple (1997) explained third space without naming it in the second edition of *Developmentally Appropriate Practice in Early Childhood Programs,* published by the National Association for the Education of Young Children (NAEYC). They said, "Some critical reactions to NAEYC's (1997) position statement on developmentally appropriate practice reflect a recurring tendency in the American discourse on education: the polarizing into *either/or* choices of many questions that are more fruitfully seen as *both/and*" (p. 23). In the new edition of that book, they integrate both/and perspectives throughout (Copple & Bredekamp, 2009).

WHAT TEACHERS CAN DO

- The first step in working toward consensus around an area of conflict is to suspend judgment and try to understand the other person's perspective. Barbara Rogoff (2003) writes: "We must separate *understanding of patterns from judgments of their value.* If judgments of value are necessary, as they often are, they will thereby be much better informed if they are suspended long enough to gain some understanding of the patterns involved in one's own familiar ways as well as in the sometimes surprising ways of other communities" (p. 14). (See Strategies 15 and 17 about patterns.)

- To suspend judgment, take the advice of Rumi, a 13th century poet from what is now Afganistan, who wrote: "Out beyond ideas of wrongdoing and rightdoing there lies a field. I will meet you there." If you go out to that field with a parent to talk about your views, you may be able to see a reality that is bigger than both of you.

- Appreciate the energy of paired truths, and remember that according to Parker Palmer (1997), only adhering to one of them is like breathing in without breathing out. Instead of trying to solve the problem right away, go out to Rumi's field, which changes the arena in which you can have a dialogue and gives you a chance to engage in holistic thinking.

- Seek an optimal response to the situation, and at the same time, increase the depth and strength of the relationship. This approach makes it easier to figure out what to do about your differences in this situation with this child and family in this classroom or program. In his foreword to *Crucial Conversations*, Steven Covey (2012) uses the term *synergy* to label third space. He says it is imperative that we nourish our relationships and develop tools, skills, and enhanced capacity to find new and better solutions to our problems. These newer, better solutions will not represent "my way" or "your way"—they will represent "our way."

- Recognize that to reach a third-space or synergistic solution you need to:
  - Believe it possible
  - Accept that there are multiple realities and paired truths
  - Change from arguing and persuading to dialoguing

- Practice dialoguing instead of arguing, because according to Steven Covey genuine dialogue "*transforms* people and relationships . . . and creates an entirely new level of bonding producing what Buddhism calls 'the middle way'—not a compromise between two opposites on a straight-line continuum, but a higher middle way, like the apex of a triangle" (p. xii).

- Recognize that, though finding a solution to the conflict is the ultimate goal, you may not reach that point, in which case you have to practice conflict *management* because you can't reach conflict resolution. Perhaps the best you can do is agree to disagree.

Once, in a workshop, the issue of differences in ideas about toilet training came up. I said, "You don't have to do what the parent wants. It's hard in a center, and I'm just telling you to be respectful of the difference." As I finished the sentence, a hand shot up from the audience. A participant was obviously very eager to speak. She stood up and said, "Here's what happened to me. A mother brought her one-year-old daughter to the center for the first time, and she told me that she was already toilet trained. I didn't believe her, but instead of responding negatively, I asked her to show me what she did. She showed me and it worked! The baby was trained and didn't need to wear diapers. It didn't take any more time and energy than changing diapers would have." What surprised me about this story was that the participant, though willing to try something new, really didn't have faith that it would work. She was wrong. It did work. This story illustrates a win-win solution. The caregiver kept on with what she believed in for the other children, but was also able to satisfy the mother. In other words, the caregiver expanded her ideas about what was possible and didn't give up anything.

22 Considering Family Participation

Sometimes called "parent involvement," family participation in schools, preschools, infant–toddler programs, and other early childhood programs can include anything from assisting in the classroom to serving on a board or advisory committee to building furniture. Other parent involvement activities can include taking equipment home to repair, washing paint smocks, contributing supplies, or coming in on a Saturday to spruce up the yard. Attending parent education sessions is yet another example of family participation. Fund-raising is still another way that families can participate. It's also important to recognize that for some families participation may mean simply getting the child up in the morning and on the bus every day. This is not the traditional approach of family members participating physically in the classroom, though even those families may be able to do something at home to send to school, such as making cookies or gathering materials for a class project.

Cooperative preschools are one example of parent participation programs and are built on parent involvement. They have been influential in getting parents whose children move on to kindergarten and the primary grades into the classrooms of their children. Without their influence, the old tradition of separating home and school would still be in effect, such as when parents sent their children off to their teachers and classrooms and neither side crossed the threshold of the other.

Traditionally, cooperative preschools have focused more on the whole of development rather than the more narrow view of school readiness or academics. That influence has brought developmentally appropriate practice into an increasing number of schools as teachers come to understand a broader definition of "readiness."

Many parent participation programs are sponsored by public school districts or linked with an adult education program. Often the parents run the program, hire the teacher, and/or sit on the decision-making board. Enrolled families usually are required to have a parent work in the classroom on a regular basis. Sometimes the parents participating that day meet after the session is over to discuss what happened. Generally, the programs have children for only half a day. These after-session meetings are part of the parent education arm of the program and are often coupled with evening meetings for the whole group. Parents who have the time and interest to be deeply involved with their children's care and education are the ones who choose this type of program.

As mentioned earlier, if the family is sending the child to public school and/or to child care while they work, they may not want or have time for required parent involvement. One of the themes of this book is to create partnerships with families, so it's important to mention that mandated parent involvement, requiring physical presence of a family member in the classroom, can work against the partnership. If one program goal is empowerment, then requiring families to do something they don't want to or don't have time for works in opposition to that goal. Anyone who is truly interested in developing partnerships with parents needs to think about how to use parent involvement toward that end rather than in a way that defeats it.

Joyce Epstein (2001), director of the National Network of Partnership Schools, breaks parent involvement into six categories of activities used by schools:

1   Parent-education activities
2   Communications between schools and families
3   Volunteer opportunities
4   At-home learning activities
5   Decision-making opportunities
6   Community collaborations

Family participation and parent involvement are behind the concept that success for the child is linked to families becoming part of the child's care and education program. Success may be defined as academic achievement, school readiness, enhanced learning, or optimal development of the whole child.

WHAT TEACHERS CAN DO

- Start at the beginning with an orientation. The enrollment paperwork should make clear the school's, classroom's, or program's philosophy about family involvement. On an ongoing basis, teachers' attitudes should be welcoming. Make parents and other family members feel comfortable whenever they enter the program.

- Set up an environment that says to family members, "You belong here." Keep diversity in mind as you do this. If possible, make a welcoming space for them. In preschool programs, it may be easier to include such things as a place for family members to sit, toys for younger siblings, and a bulletin board with items of interest for parents. If multiple languages are represented in the classroom, find ways to have the bulletin board show this fact. Some classrooms and programs have mailboxes for each family, pamphlets available (again in the languages of the families), and even books to lend that reflect diversity. A steaming coffee pot out of the reach of little hands is an added bonus.

This cooperative preschool and kindergarten brochure states that the program is child-centered but the parents own the school, so there is a constant family presence in all aspects of its operation. The parent's role is spelled out in this brochure.

Notes of appreciation are a good way to keep parents and other family members volunteering in the classroom.

Dear Mrs. Gonzalez-Mena, Thank you for correcting our seatwork, driving us to the Nut Tree and for taking our pictures. You are a superperson.

- An open-door policy lets families know that their presence is always welcome, though that may be difficult in K–3 classrooms.
- Work to develop a relationship with each family member who comes into the program. That may mean finding translators to help you communicate with some families. In preschools and infant–toddler programs, just being available when the child arrives or is picked up is a good beginning for a relationship.
- Find out the family's interests and ask how the program can serve them better. This is a good policy for programs that serve children of all ages. When the family is also a focus, instead of just the child, programs can provide or organize activities that families really want to participate in, such as excursions, parties, and Friday night pizza and video for the whole family. After this policy gets going, a parent committee can take over the planning and organizing.
- Suggest ways family members can help out or become part of the program. This works best after you get to know the family and understand their strengths, interests, and skills. You may find some families willing to share information, skills, or objects related to their uniqueness or culture, which will add richness to the children's experience.
- Offer opportunities to observe. This can be a start for parents in getting to know the program and figuring out where they best fit in as participating family members.
- Help each family get to know other families in the program.
- If parents are willing to give out contact information, create an address list to pass out.
- Notice which children spend time with each other, and tell the parents of both, in case they want to make play dates.

- Look for barriers that may be keeping some families from participating, and see which ones you can eliminate. Can younger siblings come along with the parent who wants to spend time in the classroom? Can an occasional Saturday event help the parents who want to be involved but are busy on weekdays?

- Recognize that some families see school as separate and apart from family life, and they expect teachers to do the educating without involving them. The whole idea of parent involvement may be very strange to them. Some parents may feel too inadequate to see themselves as their "child's first teacher." Don't push them to do things they feel uncomfortable doing. Just keep working on building a relationship with them.

- Look for many more ideas about how to create and support family participation in Chapters 28, 30, and 33.

Here is a story about family participation: One family felt so at home in their child care center that when the child went into kindergarten, the family welcomed the list of ways to participate that the teacher handed out the first day. This family became the catalyst for other families who weren't used to participating in their children's programs.

This family is a contrast to a family who came into the child care center with the idea that this was school and the teacher was the one who knew about education. They had great respect for this teacher—and any teacher—so they put her on a pedestal. Their attitude influenced their relationship with her. When this family met another family from their own culture who had a different idea about the child care center, they began to see a different perspective. The family they met had a cousin who was an assistant teacher in the program, and she helped them feel right at home in the center. Then, they began to notice how involved their new friends were in the program, and that gave them the idea that they could be involved too. Eventually, they started looking for ways to help out. One day, the grandmother offered to take home the paint smocks to wash over the weekend. When she brought the smocks back on Monday, she noticed a father reading a book in Spanish to a small group of children. That gave her the idea to offer to teach the children some songs and finger plays from her own childhood. Later, the mother offered to come in and make tortillas with the children. While she was there, she got the idea that maybe the center could have a potluck evening, when each family could bring an ethnic dish to share. What started as no involvement ended up as plenty of involvement, and none of it was required.

Family participation and parent involvement have been around for a long time at all kinds of early childhood programs for children from birth through age eight. One idea behind the concept is that success for the child is linked to families becoming part of their children's care and education program.

23 Including Families in the Classroom or Center

This chapter zeros in on how to use family members as volunteers in the classroom, which is a common way of getting them involved in their children's education. Head Start has used this strategy successfully since it started in the mid-sixties. Some K–3 classrooms and preschool and infant–toddler programs also use parent volunteers, but not all of them do. For some programs, it is mandated; for others, it's not.

There are many models for parent volunteers. Some cooperative preschools depend on parents as teachers to fill out adult-to-child ratios. Whether kindergarten and primary teachers use parent volunteers depends on many factors, including district policies and regulations, specialized funding, school traditions, and the teachers' own inclinations.

Having parents in the center or classroom works well when early childhood professionals are dedicated to families and view their job as family-centered care and education. It doesn't work as well when these professionals come into the field because they like working with children but dislike working with parents. In some cases, this is an early stage of professional development—the focus on children and disregard of parents—but in other cases, this attitude remains throughout the career of the professional.

Certainly, family members in the center or classroom complicate the job of the professional. For one thing, it increases the number of people and interactions. The teacher, staff, or caregiver must plan for the extra adults as well as for the children. Children can behave very differently in the presence of their parents, which can disrupt the group.

Advocates for parents in the center or classroom cite many advantages. Family members who spend time being involved in their children's education find out about what goes on in the classroom and see how their children learn. For many parents, their experience as an early learner occurred in a more highly structured, strict, academic environment, and spending time in their child's center or classroom helps them to understand developmental processes and the special approaches that work for children in their beginning years. Family members in the classroom can observe firsthand the ways their children interact with others. It broadens their view of their children. For some parents, being involved in the classroom is an eye-opening experience as they learn more about typical development.

Volunteering in the center or classroom makes parents and other family members feel good about being able to contribute to the program. The more time they spend there, the more ideas they come up with about how they can use their own talents, skills, and interests to make unique contributions. When they see other parents bring in cultural artifacts and activities, the idea spreads. Family participation can bring diversity into the classroom or center in ways that supplement what the teacher can do.

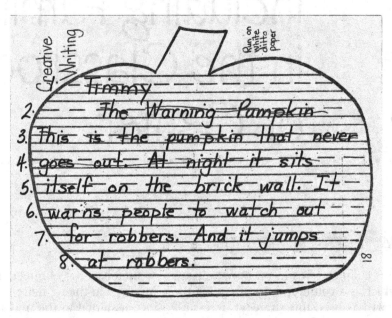

Creative Writing

Run on white ditto paper

1. Timmy
2. The Warning Pumpkin
3. This is the pumpkin that never
4. goes out. At night it sits
5. itself on the brick wall. It
6. warns people to watch out
7. for robbers. And it jumps
8. at robbers.

Parent volunteers come into the classroom to take dictation as children learn that what they say can be represented in written words. This was an October activity and represents a story by Timmy about a pumpkin. Later, he copied the story himself on another piece of paper.

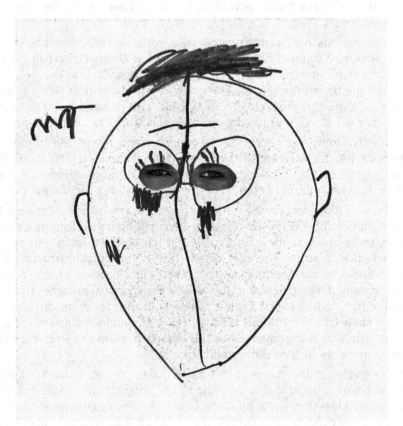

Preschoolers get more personal attention when parent volunteers are in the center encouraging the children to get involved in the various activities set out for them. A parent volunteer helped with this art project.

Feelings of security on the part of parents and children increase when parents spend time in the classroom or center. The relationships between families and staff can solidify as they get to know each other better than just the quick, daily hellos and good-byes and scattered meetings throughout the year.

WHAT TEACHERS CAN DO

- Consider instituting an open-door policy that encourages parents and other family members to feel free to visit the center or classroom at any time. For some professionals, a more specific visiting time may work better—for example, one afternoon a week family members are invited to come early and visit before their children go home. These ideas work better in programs and schools where there aren't specific requirements for outsiders in the classroom, such as having TB tests.

- When parents and other family members are coming into the classroom to assist the teacher or caregiver, it makes those family members feel more secure if they can get some kind of training —either formal or informal.

- Informal training takes into consideration what beginners need to know right away. Certainly, they need to know the expectations of the professionals and the routine of the classroom. They need a description of what they are to do and instructions or tips about how to do it. Some of these things they can learn over time, but they need definite instructions for their first day. A day of observation before they begin to actually help out can give them an idea of how things work.

- A formal training program could include an orientation to the principles, practices, and goals that relate to early childhood philosophy. Developmental information can be useful, plus some ideas about learning styles and how to respond to individual children as well as groups. Some tips on guidance approaches will help parents understand what the professional is doing and make them feel more secure when they are faced with the need to guide behavior in positive directions.

A common way of involving family members in their children's education is to invite them to volunteer in the classroom.

- Invite parents to observe. This is a very different role from helping out, and it needs to be explained to everybody—children as well as parents. It helps if there is a special badge to wear, a certain chair to sit in, or some other way of signaling that the family member is in an observation mode so that everybody understands what to expect.

- Consider other possibilities for parents in the classroom or center besides using them as helpers, assistant teachers, or observers. They can help plan and carry out special social events for special occasions or birthdays. Before instituting this idea, though, be sure that all families are okay with celebrations. Some families, for religious reasons, cannot participate in such events. Be sensitive to differences and honor them. One first-grade teacher has a different way of bringing parents into the classroom. She has parents come in twice a week for half an hour, first thing in the morning, to read to and with their children. Many of those who show up are fathers.

Focusing on Fathers and Grandfathers

24

In some families the grandparents take the place of the parents. Though this chapter focuses on fathers, keep in mind it may well be the grandfather or some other father substitute you would be trying to involve. Fathers aren't all the same. Just as there are all kinds of mothers in all kinds of situations, the same is true for fathers. Some fathers live with the mother and their children, and are closely connected; others live in the same house but are not so closely connected. Some fathers live with the other father in gay families (just as there may be two mothers in lesbian families). In any family, there may be blood ties or not. There may be marriage ties or not. Some fathers live with their children as single parents. Some fathers are raising their stepchildren as single parents. In some military families the mother is deployed overseas and the father has responsibility for the children at home. It's very hard to make a generalized statement about fathers, except to say that some early childhood education programs have a harder time involving men than they do women.

One group of fathers that may not get enough attention from early childhood professionals are those who don't live with their children. The Parent Services Project created a fatherhood project aimed at involving fathers who are not living with their children. A goal of the project was to give these fathers the support they needed to have positive relationships with their children. The project put on workshops in parenting, which included communication and conflict resolution. The fathers also learned about stress management and financial management, as well receiving job training. The outcomes of the project were remarkable; they included fewer child behavior problems, higher levels of sociability, and even a reduction in childhood poverty. Some fathers who had never had affection in their own childhood learned how to give it to their children, and they reaped the rewards of that behavioral change. Some of the fathers in this project turned their lives around, making changes that benefited themselves, their children, and their communities. As they got involved in school and other early care and education programs, they learned the importance of making time for their children.

James Levine (1993a) saw four barriers to getting men involved in Head Start and public preschool programs:

1 Father's fear of exposing inadequacies
2 Ambivalence of program staff members about father involvement
3 Gatekeeping by mothers
4 Inappropriate program design and delivery

When programs are designed for involvement by the mother rather than including both parents, men can feel uncomfortable and unwelcome. Some hints that this is

Children benefit when their fathers are part of the early care and education program. Fathers benefit, too!

happening come when teachers tend to talk to the mothers, not the fathers; when conferences are held at times when few fathers can attend; when no men work in the program; and when a child lives in two homes but only one set of newsletters and notices are sent out.

Some men arrive in K–3 classrooms and other early childhood education programs already involved in their children's lives. They've had experience in the PTA or other parent–teacher organizations as members or officers. Some have been involved with Little League as coaches. Many children enter kindergarten from Head Start, where both their parents were involved. Those experienced fathers sometimes are more easily able to involve other fathers than are the teachers or staff in the program. If you can get them organized to reach out to other men, the rate of male involvement may go up.

To get men involved in most programs, the staff has to be intentional about it. Leaving male involvement to chance almost always means that many more mothers will be involved than fathers. Stanley Seiderman, director of the Bay Area Male Involvement Network in California, had good ideas about how to make involvement in early care and education programs more attractive to men. He said, "The strongest motivators for getting and keeping fathers involved in all aspects of their child's life are expectation, encouragement and opportunity. While it is true that there are men who want to get involved and need little help to do so, most men will not usually come forward in our child care settings. They tend to be reticent and uncomfortable" (Lee, 2004).

WHAT TEACHERS CAN DO

- Make all fathers and other males feel welcome. Go back and look at Strategy 4 about creating an antibias environment. Read through each strategy, keeping a focus on fathers. Analyze an early care and education environment in terms of fathers, while keeping those strategies in mind. If you were a father, what would welcome you? What would feel less than inviting?

- While you are thinking of fathers, don't forget to consider grandfathers as well. As mentioned earlier, many grandparents are raising their children's children.

- Figure out how to get more male teachers and staff members. Explore the barriers to males entering the field, and begin to address them.

- Recognize that males experience the world differently than females do. Though early childhood professionals may strongly value gender equity, we still have to acknowledge that being a male is different from being a female.
- Analyze the environment and daily routine to see if they welcome males and reflect their interests. Also check out the curriculum and policies to be sure they are male-friendly.
- Learn more about the differences in male and female experiences by observation and discussion. One way to learn more is to increase the number of male teachers and staff members so that the numbers are more even.
- Don't assume that what you know about the differences between male and female experiences are universal. Each culture varies in what males and females experience. There is plenty to learn.
- Recognize that the field of early education and care in schools and other settings has its own culture, and that those of us who have training and experience in the field have become part of it, though we may not even be aware that it is a *culture*. Female influences have created this culture (consciously and unconsciously) more than male influences have. This is a huge emotional subject and could be debated at length.
- Learn more about the culture of early childhood education by observation and discussion. The more the culture is talked about, the more aware we will all become of it.
- Look at little things that give messages to men about their place in the program. In *Stronger Together* (2004) Lee suggests, for example, to think about the following:
  - Is the initial interview, if there is one, scheduled so that both parents can attend?
  - Does the application form ask for the name, address, and phone number of the noncustodial parent or the mother's significant other?
  - Are men on the mailing list to receive all of the announcements, invitations, questionnaires, and bulletins?
  - Are parent–teacher conferences scheduled so that both parents can come, and are both parents expected to come?
  - Can men see and interact with other men in the classroom or at the center?
- Consider these ideas for getting men into the center if hiring male teachers is difficult:
  - Male bus drivers can double as classroom aides.
  - High school and college students could volunteer as part of a class assignment.
  - Community service clubs could send males to spend time with the children.
- Decide that men want to be involved, and then proceed to include them in the decisions about *how* they want to be involved. Don't expect them to be automatically interested in everything that women teachers and mothers find engaging.
- Increase fathers' involvement in your program by using some of these ideas:
  - Create activities especially for men. For many years, Ethel Seiderman's husband Stanley held Saturday morning breakfasts for fathers at the child care center where Ethel was once director.
  - Hold an annual Father's Day picnic.
  - Have a father organize the other fathers for a workday in the center, classroom, or play yard. Mothers can be included, but if a father organizes it, men are more likely to come.
  - Research the best times to hold parent–teacher conferences so that fathers can come. Afternoons won't work for all fathers (or for all mothers).
  - Have family parties where everybody is invited, including fathers and even grandfathers.

Taking a Transformative Approach to Parent Education

25

WHAT TEACHERS NEED TO KNOW

Many people think of education as involving a teacher and a learner who each have separate roles. The teacher teaches, and the learner learns. In early childhood programs, this idea can apply to children and also to parents when the program has a parent education component. In this particular model, the learner is the parent, and the teacher is the early childhood professional or some other expert. This view of education is based on the idea that the teacher has a body of knowledge and a set of skills; the goal, therefore, is to transmit the knowledge and skills to the learner.

A different model involves a two-way process in which the roles of teacher and learner are more fluid and dynamic. This model views the teacher and learner as sharing roles. In this model, teachers are most effective when they also see themselves as learners. They get to know their students, who they are, what they are interested in, what they know and can do, what they need to know and be able to do, and how best they can learn. Teachers also learn—mostly by observing—where the "learning edge" of each student lies; that is, what each student is ready to learn next. Lev Vygotsky (1978), a Russian theorist, used the term *zone of proximal development* (or *ZPD*) for the student's learning edge.

Using these ideas of teacher as learner and student as teacher, it is possible to move away from parent education that is based on a knowledge transmission model and move toward what is called a transformative education model. In simple terms, transformative education is when two people or groups come together and, through their interactions, are both changed for the better. Transformative education, as it relates to parent education, assumes that both teacher and family have bodies of knowledge that complement each other. Transformative education is vital when diversity is present. And diversity is always present, even among groups of people who look like they are from the same background, race, or culture. Dig a little deeper, and you will find generational, religious, economic, gender, age, and ability differences, just for starters.

Transformative education doesn't preclude holding workshops, creating parenting classes, or offering books and other resources for the parents' edification. It just means that the teacher realizes there are a variety of perspectives on everything relating to education and child care. He is sensitive to differences and seeks to understand them. It's a matter of openness rather than persuasive salesmanship. Teachers can gain a great deal of knowledge themselves through a transformative education process. That knowledge can make teachers less inclined to use their power to impose their ideas and knowledge—much of which may be cultural—on families.

76

Parent education comes in many different forms. It becomes transformative when the teacher and learner share information in such a way that both learn something.

Looking at a situation where obvious diversity is present, imagine an immigrant family who is new to a school or other early care and education program. When the early childhood professional is using a transformative education model, she doesn't just set out to teach them child development or how to improve their child's academics. She also works to learn what she can about who they are and what they want for their child. She explains (through a translator, if necessary) how the program works, and she also asks about their expectations. She asks about schools and other early care and education programs in their country and how they are the same or different from here. Her motive is to discover where there's a fit, and what might cause them discomfort, in this program. She doesn't do this all at once, but slowly, over time, while working on the relationship. Both parties—the family and the teacher—gain from their many conversations and get to know each other as well. Trust builds.

It may seem like a luxury to have so many conversations with a family, but it is important to find and create opportunities to talk to families.

WHAT TEACHERS CAN DO

- Work on building a relationship with each family. Get to know them.
- Establish from the first day you meet the family and their child that you want to learn about them, including their dreams for their child and their ideas about how to fulfill them. Caution: Go slowly. Mention your goal, but before going further, consider their response. Are they suspicious, insecure, or hesitant to reply? Some families have many experiences of being questioned by authorities who had control over their lives. You want to develop a different kind of relationship, so be careful not to ask too many questions or leave them feeling like they have been interrogated.
- Keep an open mind. If a family tells you they want something that you disagree with, suspend judgment until you are sure you understand them. In the face of cultural or economic differences, misunderstandings are easy.
- Don't just ask questions. Observe as well, and comment on what you see. Sometimes asking questions doesn't work as well as just remarking about what strikes you.

- Encourage the family to observe in the classroom or program if they have time and are comfortable doing so. Ask them to comment on what they see, and listen to them with an open mind.

- Become aware of your own stereotypes, and put them aside along with your judgments. Make your goal to get to know this family uncluttered by stereotypic images.

- Notice when something a family member says or does causes you discomfort. Being aware of your own reactions gives you some clues about where you need to learn more.

- Besides your daily work and interactions with each family, put together a more formal parent education program, which can include the following:

  - Special meetings, on a topic that parents agree they want to know more about—be sure to have translators for families who need them
  - Discussion groups about issues that come up in which parents have an interest
  - Home visits, if your program or school allows it and if parents are comfortable with the idea
  - Opportunities for observation and discussion with you
  - A resource area with information that parents can use

Working with Families Around Holiday Issues

26

WHAT TEACHERS NEED TO KNOW

Many early childhood teachers love holidays and spice up their curriculum with traditional seasonal celebrations. Some even create a holiday curriculum as a main course, not just a spice. As awareness of diversity began to grow, however, some teachers began to question their holiday curriculum, because it didn't include everyone. Some then decided to expand to include different cultures and religions. That change made October through December and into January packed with holidays as teachers worked to squeeze in Columbus Day, Halloween, the Day of the Dead, Diwali, Thanksgiving, Hanukkah, Christmas, Kwanza, and Los Santos Reyes. Whew! They barely got to rest before it was Martin Luther King, Jr., Day, Chinese New Year, and then Valentine's Day.

One problem with a holiday curriculum is the mandate regarding separation of church and state. An issue with adding diversity to the holiday curriculum, even if you leave religion out, is that it is easy to pass on misinformation. Children may learn more about stereotypes than they do about true cultural differences. Another issue is that some holidays are bound to be neglected no matter how hard the teacher tries to include all cultures. It can get to be just too much! A fairly common response to the overwhelmingly diverse holiday curriculum is to eliminate *all* holidays, which some programs and schools now mandate.

Holidays bring up many issues and questions in some programs. Some questions are: Should holidays be special days or just part of the curriculum? Which way makes the holiday more culturally relevant? How do you work with parents when there is a difference of opinion?

On the positive side, holidays can be a way to involve families and to further relationships between home and school. Wonderful things can happen when parents and other family members come into the classroom to share how they celebrate a particular holiday. When teachers take into consideration the age of the children in the group and who the children are, incorporating holidays into the curriculum can be done in ways that are developmentally appropriate, relate to the educational needs of the children, help them appreciate diversity, affirm their identity, and end up being relevant and meaningful.

WHAT TEACHERS CAN DO

- Take the age of the children into consideration. The younger the child, the less meaning holidays have, and the less they learn from them. School-age children can enjoy and appreciate some disruptions in their day and are more apt to learn something from those disruptions than younger children are. For example, infants

The child who drew this may
have had Valentine's Day in
mind, but it also has a feeling
of a celebration of spring.

and toddlers feel more secure and therefore in more of a learning mode when their daily schedule stays somewhat the same. Holiday celebrations can create big disruptions, especially when there is a big fuss over them.

- Be clear about your goals for including holidays in the curriculum. If one goal is to expand an antibias curriculum, learning about and/or experiencing a wide variety of holidays can affirm cultural identity in some children and help others appreciate traditions that are different from their own.

- If another goal is to include parents in meaningful ways, holidays may be able to promote that goal. On the other hand, diverse holiday celebrations may be a deterrent to building a relationship with some parents. Get to know the families of the children in your class or group, and discover how each feels about holidays before you move forward with a holiday curriculum. Be sensitive to and respectful of families who don't celebrate any holidays, or families who worry about their children being exposed to holidays other than the ones their family celebrates.

- If you plan to include holidays, decide whether to stick to the ones represented by the families in the class or group or to introduce unfamiliar ones. It may be you have plenty of diversity and you don't need to go outside it. Or you may want to bring in something new that the children aren't familiar with, especially if it is celebrated by families in the local community, even though none of the families in your class or program celebrates it.

- Connect all holiday activities and/or lessons to real people rather than making generalizations, which can lead to stereotypes. Make sure you have accurate information.

From my own experience comes an example of a teacher who might have made a mistake around the December holidays. I can only hope that she had accurate information about the preferences of the children's families. *I remember a December math activity from the classroom of one of my sons. The children were learning about charting. That day, the teacher stood in front of the class with a piece of chart paper divided vertically down the center. Across the top was written "Christmas trees." The teacher then asked, "Who has their Christmas tree up? Raise your hand." The first column was labeled "Has Christmas tree up." Check marks were made in that column for each hand that was up. Then, the teacher asked, "Who doesn't have their Christmas tree up yet? Raise your hand." Corresponding check marks were made in the second column.* When I heard about the activity, I couldn't help but wonder how the children whose families don't celebrate Christmas felt during that activity, and what they did. Did they just keep their hands down? Did the teacher notice? Did she count to see if some hands were missing? Did some children just put their hands up anyway, even if neither question pertained to them? Obviously, the teacher made some assumptions about the religious backgrounds of the children in her class. Sometimes diversity doesn't show, but there is always diversity of some kind in any group of children and their families. Apparently, this teacher missed that concept.

Here's another example related to age appropriateness and holiday celebrations. This is about what happened on Valentine's Day in a class of three-year-olds. The teacher scheduled a party and involved the parents, who brought snacks, decorated the room and helped out. Things were going well until time to pass out valentines, at which point some children refused to give up the ones they had brought. It became an issue of "sharing" and a number of children refused. It was no longer a happy occasion! The teacher decided that the valentine cards didn't work with three-year-olds and was obviously developmentally inappropriate. In the following years she kept the party tradition, but left out the card exchange.

This story could have also related to diversity in another way. If some families had financial challenges, then teachers setting up a situation where every child was expected to bring a valentine for every other child in the class could have created a hardship for those families. It may seem as if the solution could be to have the children make the valentines at home, but even paper, scissors, glue, and crayons might have been more than some families could manage. Also some children might have considered homemade valentines inferior to commercial ones.

27

Exploring Parents' Role on Decision- Making Boards and Councils

In some schools and programs, family members serve on an advisory board or council, and in some they are the policymakers. Many elementary schools have a parent-advisory group that gives input to school policies. Preschools also involve families in an advisory capacity. Head Start is a shining example of a model that involves parents at all levels, including giving them an advisory role and, to some extent, a decision-making role. In parent participation preschools, the parent board is the decision-making body. Of course, not all schools or programs give parents this kind of power. For many, the family council is purely advisory, and professionals make the final decisions.

Having families in these advisory and decision-making roles means that the program is more likely to be responsive to diversity and to children in the ways the families wish. Community connections can be greater when parents are involved in giving advice and setting policy, which again can help the school or program be more aware of diversity. The program is more likely to be a firmer part of the community in which the families live, and to be responsive to their needs. Playing these roles helps parents and other family members see that they can influence what happens in their children's lives. The benefits go beyond their own children as they develop and hone leadership skills that serve their communities.

When families serve on boards and councils, they have a greater voice than when they come as individuals and ask that the program be sensitive to what they want for their children. The teachers and staff in a program are often from a different culture or socioeconomic level than the families they serve. These teachers and staff may not have much power themselves to apply what they know and believe using the principles and practices they've learned in their teacher preparation courses. The policies they have to follow and/or the principles and practices they've learned may set them apart from the families they serve, and communication may be blocked. Parent voices are usually quiet when they come individually—and even the loud ones eventually move on to the next grade or program. Having parent boards and councils allows voices to be heard in a different way and provides continuity as well as flexible responsiveness as the board changes over time.

This advisory group of parents and teachers meets regularly throughout the school year. This particular meeting focused on spending some money that was allocated for school improvement.

Sunny Valley School
May 13

Minutes of the Sunny Valley School Site Council meeting held on May 12.

In attendance: Sharon Allen, Latanya Miller, Sandy Smith, Dena Mundy, Sage Johnson, Dean Ames, and Juana Gomez.

The meeting was called to order at 3:39 by Chairperson Juana Gomez. Minutes of the April 14th meeting of the School Site Council were read and approved.

Latanya Miller presented the Council with two copies of the District Master Plan for School Improvement which outlines the regulations regarding all aspects of school improvement. The district has asked the site council for input concerning possible changes in the Master Plan. Site Council members were asked to review the plan and make appropriate suggestions.

Ms. Miller indicated that the School Improvement Plan budget project for the next year is $14,501, approximately 4,000 less than this year's budget. She also noted that the future of the program is still uncertain.

After a review of the district philosophy relating to student behavior, the Council discussed and composed a discipline plan for use at Sunny Valley School. The plan outlines area of responsibility for students, parents, teachers and administrators.

Ms. Miller distributed copies of the School-wide Environment component composed by the Council at the April meeting.

The meeting was adjourned at 4:43.

Dean Ames,
Secretary

Parent boards and councils benefit teachers, principals, directors, staff, and caregivers by broadening their views as they come to understand perspectives that may be different from their own. When the council or board is working well, professionals enjoy additional support that they might not otherwise experience.

Encouraging leadership among the families served will bring rich rewards. You have to get to know the families well enough to begin to discern leadership qualities. But what are those qualities? How do you know a leader when you see one? According to Debra Sullivan (2010), "Leaders are any individuals who influence others in a way that encourages them to higher or better performance and personal development. Effective leaders may or may not have authority, position, or status. They do, however, have integrity, dignity, and respect for others. Leaders empower, encourage, and support others in a shared effort to achieve goals or create change.... They take action where action is needed and they enable others to take action when another person's strengths and ability are needed" (p. 7).

WHAT TEACHERS CAN DO

- Help each family understand how the program, organization, or school works so that they have a bigger picture than if they only tuned into their own and their child's experiences with the caregiver, staff, or teacher.
- Look at your own attitudes. (See Strategy 7, Removing Barriers to Partnerships.) Openness to parents' perspectives is essential for working with parent boards and councils.
- Learn to look for leadership qualities, even in shy, quiet people. Who has vision? Who wants to make something happen? Who has influence on others? Who can work both independently and interdependently? These qualities may not show up readily. You may have to look hard for them, but you will be richly rewarded

as you become increasingly aware of people with leadership potential among the families.

- Mentor new leadership. Encourage and give support to these potential leaders. Provide training for them. Head Start is known for developing leaders—not only in the program, but also in the community. A common Head Start story is the bringing up of parents through the ranks of the profession, starting as a parent volunteer and eventually working as a staff member, a teacher, or even a director or other administrative position.

Part of the process of creating a board or council is recruiting parents. Individual parent voices may be ignored but when parents come together on parent boards and councils their voices may command more attention.

28 Creating Environments for Communication

An environment influences behaviors as well as shapes thoughts and creates feelings in people—both adults and children. We behave one way in a library, another way in a bank, a different way in a workout room, and yet another way in a place of worship. The environment gives us messages about how to behave. Part of growing up is learning how to read those messages. Early childhood professionals are aware of this phenomenon and often take care to arrange their environments so that children get the right messages about how they should behave there. Take a library space in a classroom, where the goal is to settle down and enjoy books—the area is set up to be comfortable, cozy, relaxed, and relatively quiet. That library corner is a contrast to the play space in an infant center, where physical exploration is a goal and the room is set up to encourage children to move freely rather than snuggle in.

It may not be easy to set up environments that invite parents into the classroom or center, but when it is possible, it's a worthy goal. In any program, the entry space can give a welcoming message. If the space is limited, it might be a simple message, such as a bulletin board with pertinent items displayed. The most likely place to see more elaborate environmental arrangements for parents is in a preschool or infant center, where family members deliver and pick up their children. Some programs have cubbies that family members can use for messages or notices. Of course, a couple of comfortable chairs, a table, a coat rack, and a steaming pot of coffee (out of reach of the children) are other welcoming devices. For parents who bring younger siblings with them to pick up their children, some readily available, simple toys or baby books are welcoming, too. If parents spend time in the program itself, either as observers or as volunteer helpers, another welcoming sign is a place for parents to safely store their belongings. An example of a strong environmental invitation in an infant center would be a place for breast-feeding mothers to feel relaxed and comfortable. The message here is that they are welcome to come in to feed their babies.

Many environmental factors, besides lack of space or funding for adult furniture, work against inviting parents. If children are bused, the families may not come on a daily basis, but only for enrollment procedures, conferences, meetings, or open houses. The spaces for these events may be functional but usually are not very warm and welcoming. That's the common situation. It is hoped that this chapter will get you thinking beyond *what is* in order to start conceiving of *what can be*. Until early childhood professionals raise their sights and envision better spaces than are the norm, there isn't much hope for change. Much of this book is based on visions and hopes for change.

A note: This chapter is about physical environments for communication, and as such has more to do with programs for children younger than six. Preschool and school are usually quite different in many ways, including physical environments. As we all know, there are also electronic environments for communication, and those will be discussed in chapters 30 and 31.

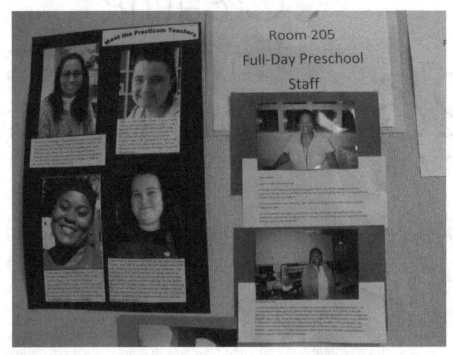

Help parents and other family members get to know the teacher and staff of the classroom by putting up a bulletin board with pictures and information.

WHAT TEACHERS CAN DO

- Analyze the environment you are in right now, and think about how it affects your behaviors, thoughts, and feelings.

- Analyze the early childhood environment you are most familiar with, and figure out what messages it may be giving parents. Try to imagine yourself as a parent bringing your child into the classroom. Think about what environmental arrangements could be made to make you feel welcome.

- Think about ways the families can see themselves and other families represented in the physical environment. Consider family photos, artifacts, and signs in the languages of the families.

- Help parents get to know the teacher and staff of the classroom or center by putting up a bulletin board with pictures of anyone who works with their children. Include their names, what they want to be called, and a short biography. Getting to know who is in and around their child's classroom helps parents feel more secure and at home.

- If parents only come occasionally, be sure that when they do they feel welcome in the spaces they visit. Put some thought into those spaces.

- Consider the entryway. What is there that gives these messages: "Welcome. Come in. Make yourself at home"?

- Consider the registration and reception areas. Do parents feel they belong there? What signs tell you that other family members are welcome? Are there toys for children while their parents sign up or sign in? Is the area wheelchair accessible? Is there evidence of what kind of program this is, such as child-centered decorations or products? Does the area take aesthetics into consideration?

- Consider the furniture arrangements. In the office, is the visitor's chair across from the desk where the principal or director sits? Though you may not be able to suggest it, even such a simple device as moving the chair out from behind the desk and next to the visitor's chair changes a formal atmosphere to a warmer, friendlier one.
- How much of the natural environment is visible? Is there natural lighting, with windows looking out at trees or plants? Is there an outdoor area for parents to make themselves comfortable?

29 Empowering Self and Others

What does empowerment mean? That depends on your definition of power. If you equate power with control and domination, then empowerment of parents and family members doesn't make sense. To consider a different definition, look to the origins of the word *power*, which comes from the Latin root meaning "to be able." Looking at it in that sense suggests what is sometimes called *personal power*. Personal power can be defined as the ability to be who you really are. Intisar Shareef, a community college professor, takes personal power a step further and considers it to be the ability to define your own reality and have others accept it. Her definition takes power beyond the personal and into the interpersonal—indeed, into the political realm. I see personal power as what is behind interpersonal and political power. All these aspects of power are important, and none need have anything to do with domination.

Watch the interactions between two people closely; sometimes their body language tells you that one is trying to dominate the other. Here is an example of such an interaction: *A parent storms into the director's office after pushing aside a secretary who tries to stop him. He strides across the room and stands with his hands on the director's desk. He leans way over so that his face is close to hers and says, "My child is a vegetarian and your teachers are feeding her meat!" His expression bristles with rage as he waits for her response. Note how both his verbal and nonverbal communication put him in the top-dog position—just like in a real-life dogfight, where one dog dominates the other. This human interaction is about winning and losing. The parent is out to win the fight, and depending on how the director responds, he just may intimidate her enough to consider himself the winner.* This may be dog nature, but it isn't human nature—it is learned. And anything that is learned can be unlearned. Empowering parents and other family members is about helping them find and use their personal and interpersonal power, and avoid using dominant and submissive behaviors.

Some people enjoy jockeying for power. Two people who are equally good at playing the dominating game may switch positions throughout an interaction, leaving no clear winner at the end. Even if one wins, the loser may enjoy the game enough to keep playing it the next time they interact. Other people don't jockey for position but immediately make themselves submissive when interacting with someone who is even a little dominating. Let's look at an example of how that works. The issue is the same but this time it is a different parent: *A mother comes into the office after learning that her vegetarian child is being given meat in the child care center. She stops at the secretary's desk and asks to see the director. The secretary says that the director is on the phone and that she will have to wait in the hall outside the office because there is no room for her inside. The mother retreats to the hall and finds that the only chair is a child's chair. She sits down on it. After 15 minutes, she checks with the secretary, who apologizes for forgetting her and ushers her into the director's office. The director sits behind a rather large desk, where he is reading some papers, and doesn't look up when the mother enters. The mother stands silent, shifting her weight from foot to foot. The director finally looks up, paper still in hand, and murmurs "Yes?" before looking back down at the paper. The person with the power in this situation is the director. We don't know if the mother made herself submissive or was forced into the role by the secretary's and director's actions. If being the underdog is her usual role, it's possible that she'll switch roles in interactions with people she perceives as weaker than herself—such as children.*

Notice the gender stereotyping in these two stories—both have a male dominating a female. As an interesting exercise, try switching genders in these two stories; see if you can imagine them that way.... Did you learn anything by doing that?

WHAT TEACHERS CAN DO

- Recognize that domination is not natural but is learned. Furthermore, systems of domination are supported by the institutions of society. That means that not everyone is born with the same chance to win in the domination game. Groups targeted for bias on the basis of race, culture, gender, age, class, ability, or sexual orientation have a harder time dominating than do those who enjoy the privileges that society automatically gives them. Not that all people in nontargeted groups play the domination game, but if they do, it is easier for them to win than it is for people in targeted groups, especially if those in the targeted groups have internalized their oppression. Of course, not all people in targeted groups submit to domination. Many are outstanding game players, but even if they are good enough to win, institutionalized bias makes sure that they never get in a position to play the dominating game with those who control the institutions. Until we all recognize how the domination system operates, and then work to dismantle it, we won't be fully effective at empowering children and their families.

Empowerment is contagious. This child shows evidence of feeling empowered.

- What professionals can do is help family members tap into their personal power—the form of power that everyone has. When personal power is acknowledged and nourished, people are able to show who they really are. They don't need to dominate others, and they can resist being put in a submissive position through internalized oppression (when the messages of the oppressor guide the person from the inside).

- Help family members "find their voice," which is the way people express their personal power.

- Empower yourself. Start by becoming aware of how you react to perceived threats by becoming defensive. If the director in the story above had responded to the dominating father by meeting him head-on or putting up a protective shield, the result would have been blocked communication. If instead she brought her personal power to the situation, she could have responded as her authentic self and given a nondefensive reaction, perhaps surprising the father out of his dominating stance.

- A book by communications expert Sharon Ellison called *Taking the War out of Our Words: The Art of Powerful Nondefensive Communication* (2009) has a number of suggestions for responding to power that comes in the form of domination. She lists many strategies, including recognizing and stepping back from defensive feelings, gathering information to get the story straight, expressing personal reactions with integrity and passion, and setting limits non defensively. Very few people come by these approaches naturally, so Ellison urges readers and trainees to regard these strategies as skills that need to be learned and practiced.

30 Communicating Through Writing

Attempts should be made to communicate with family members in every medium possible. Writing is one major way to get messages across. Throughout the history of early childhood education, teachers and families have communicated with each other through writing.

Although not yet universal, electronic means of communication have become a major way of communicating with many families. Notes, messages of concern, requests to make appointments, newsletters, articles, and most things that used to go home on paper can now be sent electronically. This is especially useful in corporate child care programs, where such communication can be timely and immediate, and is especially useful if children and families are located in the same building. Be considerate about flooding families with too much—a problem with technology. In the past, the problem was not enough communication; now, it is so easy to send an e-mail with an attachment that it is sometimes overdone.

Attempts should be made to communicate with family members in every medium possible. Written notices are one important way to get messages across.

This letter goes home to families the first week of school. It is intended to give them a brief introduction to the classroom that will tide them over until Back-to-School Night.

First Grade
Ms. Ritz
Monte Vista School

First grade is an exciting year because children expand their learning incredibly, exert their competence and and develop independence. My goals for all children are to

- support learning by assessing the appropriate activities that will challenge children without discouraging them;
- encourage children to find their strengths so they can feel proud of their accomplishments;
- help children find strategies to become self-motivated learners.

This is a "Can Do" classroom. First graders can do lots of things!

Behavior:

Lifeskills teach children the language of responsible behavior. Our classroom will use Lifeskills, I messages, a Peace Table and Classroom meetings to make sure students have all the knowledge needed for successful behavior.

No one's perfect. On horrible, no good, very bad days, anyone might need some time out. In our class it is called Australia. Children who are sad, angry, etc. can spend a few minutes quietly there to regroup for learning.

For problems between peers the Peace Table is a place to give and receive I messages without disturbing others.

Repeated disruptive behavior that interferes with learning can occur. Children will bring home a Lifeskill Homework note. Please discuss the problem, suggest some strategies or solutions, sign and return.

I'm sure you'll have questions and concerns as time goes on. Please communicate any concerns as they arise. Ask questions, share ideas, offer help. These are ways to get in touch with me:

- You can send a note in your child's folder.
- Leave a post- it on the "moon table" during Family Reading.
- Phone the school: 792-4531.
   If it can't wait until the next day, call my home before 9 pm: 578-8052.
- Send me e-mail: kritz414@sbcglobal.net

Let's have a great year!

It's important to become sensitive to what it is like not to understand what is going on. I had a lesson once when I attended a lecture on bilingual education. The speaker started out speaking in a language no one in the audience understood. He went on and on for what seemed like half an hour, though it was only 10 minutes. The audience immediately drifted off and stopped paying attention. Finally he switched to English, and asked us, "How many of you thought what I said was important." Nobody raised a hand. He went on, "You figured if it was important for you to know, I would have found a way to tell you—right?" We nodded in agreement. "You have just had the experience of an immigrant family who doesn't speak English. That lecture reminded me of a mother of a child in my preschool class. One time she told me how easy life was before she learned to read English. She had a number of children in school and notes would come home on a regular basis. She'd just throw them away. She said that she figured if they said anything important someone would let her know. Once she learned to read English she was shocked to discover how much she had been missing and the hardships her children had suffered because she threw all those notes away.

Ideally, every classroom would have a family center like this one does—where families have access to a computer and other resources.

WHAT TEACHERS CAN DO

- Let's start with diversity. Recognize that not all families have literacy skills. Those families need verbal communication, either by telephone or face-to-face. Also, not all families speak, let alone read and write, English, so any communication with them needs to be in their home language.

- Communication about each child should go to families daily when possible.

- Use electronic means of communication. E-mail is one. Family all-inclusive websites between the school or center and families is another. Blogs and other social media can be useful. But don't use electronic methods exclusively. Although most people who don't have a computer can use one at the local public library, some will still lack access to electronic communication. Be sure to use other means to reach families who either don't have or don't use computers or other electronic devices regularly.

- Use personal notes to communicate about a variety of things. If you don't want to e-mail, it doesn't take long to jot down a brief note on a piece of paper and send it home with the child. Subjects for notes can be positive comments about the child, something he or she did or said, and your appreciation of some contribution he or she made to another child or to the class. Of course, thank-you notes to family members for their contributions are not only a social nicety but also a way to let families know they are appreciated.

- "Happy-grams" are easy-to-use, commercial notes to send home bits of good news about a child. Usually, they have smiley faces and a place to fill in blanks. You can also make them by hand—you don't need commercial ones. These can be a real bonus for families who are used to notes coming home about misbehavior instead of good news.

- The opposite of happy-grams for some families may be assessment reports. For kindergarten and primary students, these may be in the form of report cards or test results. Certainly, it's better for any assessment results to be discussed with families in person rather than sent home electronically or on a piece of paper, but the reality is that such things do happen.

- Communicate with families through newsletters. Newsletters help families know what is going on in the classroom. They can be physical or electronic. Having an idea of recent themes, activities, and events helps them talk to their children about their experiences. Newsletters also clue family members in about upcoming events. They can serve as a means of connecting families to each other, especially when they contain news items pertaining to families. Other uses of newsletters can be to help families understand the purposes of various activities and give ideas for carrying on at home themes and activities that originate in the classroom. Newsletters can also ask for ideas from families, and thus become a two-way communication device.

- Bulletin boards are another way of communicating through writing. Some families who don't interact much with the teacher or staff may use bulletin boards as important sources of information. Here are some ideas for their effective use:
  - Put bulletin boards in a location where they are clearly visible and accessible.
  - Label the bulletin board so that families know it is for them. Make it attractive and keep it up to date. If it always looks the same, families will stop looking at it.
  - Items on the bulletin board should respond to the specific interests of the families enrolled.
  - The bulletin board can include such items as recipes for play dough, guidelines for choosing books or toys, announcements of coming events, and lists of community resources.
  - Pertinent articles of interest to families are useful. If the article is short, it can just be posted. If the article is longer, copies should be available for family members to take home.

- Some programs have a daily bulletin—often hand printed on a white board—that gives families who pick up their children the highlights of what went on that day. This bulletin is more timely than a newsletter and more visible than an item on a bulletin board. Such a device can provide families with conversation starters when they talk to their children. The question "What did you do today?" sometimes is answered with "Nothing." It often works better to mention something specific, such as "How did you like making tortillas today?"

- Consider using two-way journals. This written device is especially effective in infant–toddler programs, where daily two-way communication is vital in order to meet the child's needs. A two-way journal is used during the day by the staff to record events and details of caregiving, from amounts eaten to diaper contents and changes. Of course, other items of interest can also be included. At the end of the day, the journal goes home with the family, and they record what caregivers need to know the next day—how well the baby slept, when he or she ate, and any notable differences in routine. Mood changes can be indicators of the onset of illness and should be noted as well.

- Some programs have a family library and make books and articles available to borrow. Ideally each classroom would have a family center where families have access to computers and school or center information and resources.

- Some programs collect pamphlets from community resources and make copies available to families.

- Get creative and involve children in your communication efforts with their family. One example used in kindergarten by the teacher of one of my grandchildren involved a traveling teddy bear that was accompanied by a journal intended to record his adventures in each home he visited. The bear and the journal came in a backpack and went home with a different child each weekend. The idea was for a family member to read parts of the journal to the child and help him or her write additional journal entries, which could be dictated by the child and written by a family member.

This communication is designed to involve families at home in working on specific skills that the child needs at school.

To the folks at _____
house,
    Your child needs extra practice in
_____.
Please spend some time working with your child on this skill. A little attention now will make a big difference later on.
    Thanks,
        KITTY KITZ

31 Holding Ongoing Conversations with Families

· ·

WHAT TEACHERS NEED TO KNOW

Finding time to talk with families is not an easy task for early childhood professionals, even for those working in programs serving children under school age. It is even harder for those who work in schools. When children come on a bus, or walk to school on their own, teachers may not even see the parents. In fact, it may be next to impossible for teachers and families to have ongoing personal conversations, but electronic conversations can substitute. When teachers value communication with families, they work harder to figure out how to do it than when they don't see the importance of teacher–family contact.

Ongoing face-to-face conversations between teachers and families are easier in those pre-kindergarten programs where parents or other family members arrive with their children and return to pick them up. That means that they see each other, but it is usually at a busy time for everybody. Having a chat may be difficult if parents are in a hurry or come back tired at the end of the session or day. Even so, teachers and caregivers shouldn't wait for the perfect opportunity.

Daily conversations can be an important way to get to know each other. In many programs, these conversations are the main form of parental involvement and serve the important function of making the parent a part of the program. It can be a time to exchange information on child- and family-related issues.

Not every school sees parents on a daily basis, but some have a policy that a family member must take their child to the classroom to ensure daily contact between the teacher and a family member. When family members don't come to the school or program, electronic communication and telephone conversations can supplement face-to-face contact. Use these conversations to ask about absenteeism or to share a personal observation or anecdote about the child. Although it may be difficult to accept calls or answer e-mails from families during working hours, letting them know what times are best to call gives them the possibility of initiating a conversation. Some teachers make themselves available for telephone conversations on a regular basis, and let families know when that time is—nap time is a favorite among child care providers and all-day preschool teachers.

Home visits are a wonderful way for teachers and families to talk to each other. Seeing families on their own turf makes for a much better relationship. In some programs home visits are built in. Meeting families in their work settings is another way to get better acquainted and exchange information. That won't work for everybody, but when it can work, it can be a real bonus.

WHAT TEACHERS CAN DO

- Greet parents by name every time you see them, and make a point to say good-bye. If you can squeeze in a conversation after the greeting or before the good-bye, family members will feel more valued. That's the way to grow a relationship.

- Make positive remarks about their child whenever you talk to or communicate in other ways with the family.

- If the child is present, include him or her in the conversation. It's disrespectful to talk around children as if they don't exist.

- The attitude of the professional gives messages about whether it's okay to have a conversation or if this is just a quick encounter. Try to *unbusy* yourself when family members arrive. It isn't easy when you have a group of children you are responsible for, but it is worth doing.

- If you have problems making yourself available for more than a hello and good-bye, try to figure out a way to do so. Make yourself available, even if it isn't easy. Here are some ways to do this:
  - Suggest that parents visit or observe, and then make time to talk to them.
  - Stagger arrival and departure, if possible, so that everybody doesn't arrive and leave at once.
  - Have an extra staff person come in during the times that parents are there.

- Although some teachers separate their private lives from their professional lives, others who live in the same neighborhood take time to talk when they run into family members of the children in their center, family child care home, or school.

Keeping in touch with families through regular conversations with them is important. It isn't always easy to find time, but this director is making time for a quick chat with a baby and hopefully also the mother.

- Consider home visits if the program permits and parents are comfortable with them.
- Schedule conferences and meetings with families, either individually or in groups.
- Keeping records of contacts with parents helps professionals discover if they are neglecting some families.

Here is a story: A lonely grandfather who came to pick up his granddaughter stayed and stayed. The family child care provider had to move him toward the door so that she could get on with her work. One day, he remarked about the piano in the provider's family room. She asked if he played, and he replied that he did. She invited him to play something for the children. After that, he came on a regular basis and stayed for a half hour playing for the children. Eventually, he started giving lessons to some of the children. Everybody was happy about the arrangement.

Looking at Nonverbal Communication Across Cultures

32

Nonverbal behavior is like a secret code that is understood but not talked about. Meaning never comes in words alone, but also relates to posture, movement, facial expressions, eye movements, gestures, and how close or how far away we stand. We must be able to pick up silent messages sent alone or together with words. We read these messages effectively every day, except when we meet someone who has a different system of nonverbal communication. That's when miscommunication occurs.

For example, miscommunication may occur when someone from Mexico watches an Anglo explaining a child's height by holding a hand out with the palm down. Although this gesture is easily understood by many people in the United States, a person from Mexico might find it very strange, because that particular gesture is only used for measuring objects. To measure people, the index finger is pointed up at the appropriate height. This may not be a big issue, and it perhaps will be laughed off by the Mexican person. Nevertheless, the message received is different from what was intended.

A bigger issue occurs when a teacher touches a child on the head and the parent worries that the gesture has stolen the child's spirit. Some people from Southeast Asia attach deep significance to a hand on the head. To other people, touching someone on the head is a sign of affection and a way they express love or comfort to dogs or children. Most of those people would never touch adults above the shoulders, however, and would not touch the president of the United States at all, except to shake his hand if it were offered. Rules about touching are governed by status and power issues and are tied to respect. How, when, where, and why we touch each other is cultural. No one explains the rules, but we learn them. Cultural learning is subtle and starts very early.

Touching patterns vary greatly from culture to culture. A huge problem can occur when a touching pattern in one culture is regarded as inappropriate, sexual, or downright abusive in another culture. In the United States we have laws against abuse, and cross-cultural touching patterns could get people arrested if what was intended were taken the wrong way.

Touch is just one example of a cultural difference that affects communication. Personal space is another. How close we stand or sit and whether we breathe on people we are talking to hold cultural meaning. A person who comes from a "close culture" feels she is being shunned when someone from a more distant culture backs off. The person backing off may feel crowded and find the experience awkward or offensive, and she may even feel afraid. If she feels angry, she may be tempted to say, "Get out of my face!" Yet the person who comes too close in the name of friendliness may feel that the person

These two seem to be doing just fine reading each other's nonverbal communication, but they could have a problem if one moves in closer or the other steps back. The amount of personal space an individual feels comfortable with is just one aspect of nonverbal communication.

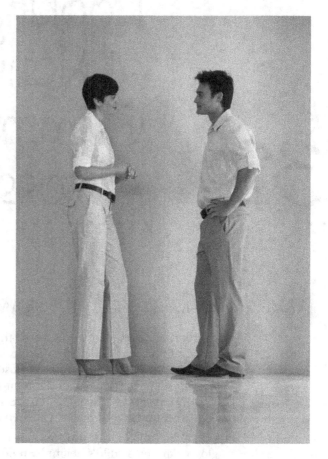

who is backing off is either weird or a cold, uncaring person. Each reads the message from the other in a way that is different from what was intended.

Eye contact is another example of a cultural difference. Learning about eye contact patterns starts in infancy. For example, in cultures where babies are constantly carried on their mothers' backs, intimacy is not necessarily expressed by eye-to-eye gaze. One common pattern of eye contact in the United States is for the listener to look directly at the speaker, and for the speaker to gaze into the listener's eyes but also look away occasionally. Someone with this pattern who talks to someone with a different eyecontact pattern may feel uncomfortable. He may even regard the listener who doesn't look at him as shifty, dishonest, or disrespectful. "Look at me when I talk to you" is sometimes heard from teachers whose students' eye contact patterns don't match their own. The listener who is expressing respect by keeping his eyes lowered or looking elsewhere when being spoken to may be mystified by the speaker's reaction to this eye contact pattern.

"Don't stare!" is a cultural command to children, but this is not a universal no-no. In some cultures, it's not only polite to stare but expected. A member of a staring culture feels rejected when no one stares at him. In other cultures, staring is not only impolite but can be considered downright dangerous.

WHAT TEACHERS CAN DO

- Become consciously aware of nonverbal behaviors. Although you may be used to reading messages that come from posture, movement, facial expressions, eye movements, gestures, and relative distance, realize that across cultures these behaviors don't necessarily mean the same thing. Look for communication problems below the level of words and their meanings. The goal is to expand your ability to pick up silent messages in the ways they are intended.

- Recognize your own patterns of nonverbal behavior. Most of us are not conscious of these until we meet someone whose patterns don't match ours. Consider that even though your own nonverbal behavior patterns may feel right, normal, or good, it doesn't mean that they are in any way superior to another person's patterns.

- Recognize that learning unwritten cultural rules of nonverbal communication takes time and patience. The best approach is to be aware of differences and to read the feedback from the parent or family member exhibiting them. Try different approaches if you are picking up discomfort in your attempts to communicate. You can ask. You may have to begin to develop the skills of an anthropologist to do this observing and asking, but those skills will serve you well.

- Sometimes you can talk about subtle behavior differences, but it takes sensitivity to bring them out without causing further discomfort and perhaps defensiveness. Having a relationship with the parent or family member you are talking to can help bring the issues to the surface and make those issues easier to discuss.

- Don't expect that just because you know a person's culture you can predict his or her behavior. Few cultural patterns are rigid or apply to all members of a culture. Furthermore, cultural patterns change when they come in contact with new patterns.

- Recognize that within a culture, body language may vary by age, status, and gender.

- A classic book which may take you further in your studies of nonverbal behavior is *The Silent Language* by Edward T. Hall. The book cover says, "The spoken language is only one means of communication...a leading anthropologist reveals how people 'talk' to each other without the use of words."

33 Meeting with Families for the First Time

Laying the foundation for a relationship starts when parents first meet the teacher, provider, director, or caregiver. The meeting is different depending on whether the family is going to their local neighborhood public school or is choosing the program or family child care home from a number of available ones. Sometimes there is no choice, and the family is just glad to be accepted in the only program for which they qualify.

The first encounter with the family sometimes involves a good deal of information and paperwork. Besides the usual address, phone number, and general information, there may be health history forms, emergency contact forms, and others related to registration. For a program like Head Start there may be forms related to the family income level and forms to be signed acknowledging that the staff is required to report any suspected child abuse. This first meeting may or may not involve the teacher. The paperwork makes an unfortunate beginning if the emphasis is to be on human relationships.

The first gathering may be a group meeting with all the families who are enrolling their children. Hopefully the group is just made up of the families who are in the same class, rather than the whole school, and it's taking place in the classroom, not the multipurpose room. If filling out forms and receiving informational papers was done at registration, then this is a get-acquainted meeting—not only with the teacher(s) and classroom, but also with other parents. Helping families to get to know each other can big a big bonus for everybody!

In some programs, the first meeting with the family may be in their own home. Home visits, not just at the beginning but throughout the year, have long been a valuable part of early childhood education programs, though mostly in Head Start and some other preschools. There are many obstacles to teachers making home visits, but also many advantages if these obstacles can be overcome. Some advantages are seeing a child in the context of home and family and gaining a better understanding of who that child is. Home visits can give information about the child's interests, skills, and learning styles. Meeting the family on their own territory can solidify the relationship with the teacher and help that teacher see how the family members and child interact at home. In addition, the teacher can meet family members who never come to the school or center, and learn about the resources they have to offer the program.

When parents and professionals can just talk together and share information, they are off to a better start. Of course, it is useful to have parents fill out a form that lets them explain their child's particular needs, ways of expressing herself, and other important information. Parents also usually are grateful for written information about the program, although they may prefer to take it home to read. Of course, if the families speak languages other than English, all paperwork should be translated and someone should be there at the meeting to translate orally as well. If the meeting is designed to be comfortable, relaxing, and not overwhelming, it's a better start. Additionally, when a separate meeting is set up for each family, it creates a good chance to begin a relationship.

Here is a fairly simple and straightforward form that supplies basic information about the family and the child and invites family members to volunteer in the classroom. It also gives the option of doing work at home for the class. Notice that the form asks for "parent(s) name(s)," not mother's and father's names, which makes it appropriate for single-parent families and also for families with parents of the same sex.

Home/School Connection

Child's Name _____ Birthday _____

Parent(s) Name(s) _____

Siblings (names and ages) _____

_____

Address _____

Home Phone # _____ Work Phone # _____

Pets (kind/name) _____

Hobbies/Interests _____

_____

Name you want your child to learn to write:

First: _____ Last: _____

Some things you may want to know about my child: (use back if necessary)

_____

_____

_____

Are you interested in volunteering in the classroom? _____
Times of Availability: M _____ T _____ W _____ T _____ F _____

Are you interested in doing work at home? _____

Programs for children age five and under sometimes have a parent handbook that contains information the parents need. The table of contents for this parent handbook, from a developmental children's center, shows that it is full of specifics that many families will appreciate having in writing.

TABLE OF CONTENTS

WHAT TEACHERS CAN DO

- Find out right away what the family members want to be called and what they want you to call their child. Learn to pronounce names correctly. Tell them what you want to be called. Be aware of cultural differences in the use of names and titles. Some families may feel uncomfortable calling you by your first name, and even more uncomfortable letting their child do so. Some families may want their child to call you "teacher" without using your name, which to you may feel uncomfortable but for them is an appropriate sign of respect for your position.

- If this is a preschool or kindergarten class, discuss possible separation issues the child might have when starting the program. Of course, separation issues might also arise among older children, especially if they are new to the school. Share ideas with the parents, and listen to theirs about how to help their child cope with feelings about separation.

- For the youngest children, having the first meeting in their own home allows them to meet the new adult in their life on their own turf. In most cases, that is difficult, but when it works out, there are a number of benefits for both the child and the family.

- If possible, invite the child and a family member to visit the program before the child actually starts. This pre-entry visit can ease the parents' minds as they watch the teacher interact with the child and see how things work in the program. It can also relieve children's anxieties to some extent.

- If the children are young and are all starting the program at the same time, staggering their entry can help them get more adult attention than if the whole group arrives the first day at the same time.

It is important to prepare parents for the separation difficulties their children might have when they first start in a program.

- Ideally, the first days should be short ones. That is not always possible, but it is worth considering.

- Although some programs have a policy about parents not staying in the classroom while their children are first adjusting, there are advantages to having a different policy. When parents ease their children into a program and are there for them at first, it not only sets a tone of welcome for the parents and their involvement, but also makes the transition easier for the child.

- Recognize that it's quite natural for some parents to have strong feelings about being separated from their children. Empathize with those parents, and avoid judging them as being too attached or overprotective. Parental emotions can be complicated and intense. They may experience feelings of ambivalence about leaving their children, worries about safety and quality of care, and fears about their child becoming attached to someone else.

- For those parents who have never separated from their child until this point, it may be helpful for them to know about the kinds of behaviors that are common in children. When this subject is discussed openly, it can relieve parents' minds that the early childhood professional isn't judging them or their child. Separation behaviors in young children can include:
  - Crying, clinging, and protesting
  - Increased dependence
  - Difficulty in eating
  - Fears about going to sleep
  - Regressive behaviors—going back to an earlier stage in their lives, such as wetting their pants or sucking their thumb
  - Passive behavior, as if they aren't quite "there."

34 Thinking About Meetings in General

WHAT TEACHERS NEED TO KNOW

Many types of meetings for parents can occur in early care and education programs. There are, of course, specific kinds of meetings, such as conferences. The first meeting with a family is another specific kind. This chapter is about meetings in general, which can include parent discussion groups, informal support groups, planning meetings for fund-raising, planning meetings for field trips, board or council meetings, reading and study groups, and any other kind of meeting you can think of. Sometimes parents get together regularly to do crafts and talk.

Meetings are more effective if they are planned around what the families think they need, rather than around what teachers think the families need. When parents and other family members have a chance to express what they want and share their interests, they may be more inclined to attend meetings. It's best if families choose and guide the agenda of meetings.

If some of the meetings are designed as "parent education," be sure that the format is an interactive one rather than the delivery of information from some expert. Although lectures may be interesting to some parents, this format fails to acknowledge that those in the audience have expertise as well. Delivering information in ways that ignore the competencies of the parents leads the relationship between staff and families away from partnerships.

WHAT TEACHERS CAN DO

- Before you start planning meetings do some informal "anthropological research." Ask people from different cultures what kinds of meetings appeal to them. Find out what has bothered them in the past about meetings they have been to. Ask other experienced teachers their ideas for incorporating diversity in meetings. Try to be guided by what you learn.

- Plan the size and style of the meeting so that it meets the parents' needs for comfort and provides an opportunity to talk with each other. Small groups create feelings of closeness, community, and ownership of the meeting. Meetings of one classroom or center are more effective than meetings of a whole school.

- Select a good time for the meeting. Get family input about the best date and time. Some parents find it enticing to come after work and have supper provided, followed by the meeting. Other parents who work close by can do "brown-bag" meetings at lunchtime.

- Provide child care, if needed.

Many types of meetings for parents can occur in early care and education programs.

- Be clear about the purpose of the meeting. If appropriate, provide the families an agenda beforehand. Leave space on it so you can get their input either before or during the meeting. If articles or other information are appropriate and related to the purpose of the meeting, distribute them beforehand as well.

- Consider involving the children in making invitations, decorations, or refreshments for the meeting.

- Try to create a warm, friendly atmosphere where people feel like sharing.

- Use name tags if the parents don't know each other.

- Use icebreakers to help participants get acquainted with each other. Some kind of active exercise can help participants feel comfortable and relaxed. It creates a conducive atmosphere for interaction and sets a tone for the meeting.

- Plan meetings to encourage interaction among the participants. Discussions work better than lectures.

- Bring in interpreters, if needed, so that everyone understands all that is said. You can also ask families to bring their own interpreters. Of course, all written material distributed beforehand and at the meeting should be translated into the languages represented in the class.

- Consider your role in the meeting. If you can be a facilitator rather than the person in charge, it's more likely that participants will interact with each other. As a facilitator, your role can be to provide some structure and ensure that everybody gets to talk.

- Don't think you have to be the only one planning and facilitating meetings. Let the families create a committee that takes over that job, or share the responsibility with them.

- Icebreakers for parent meetings can include:
  - Play the "name game." Use a lightweight ball or a soft, throwable object for this icebreaker. Say the name of a participant, and then toss him or her the ball. Tell that participant to do the same until all the participants have been named aloud.
  - Pair up participants with people they don't know and give them a few minutes to get acquainted with their partner. Have them introduce each other to the group.

Date _____

Dear _____,

   I really want you to come
to see _____
_____
in Room 28. Please come
Tuesday, _____
from 7:45 to 8:15 a.m.

   Love,

     _____

Estimada/o _____

Deseo que Ud. venga al "Open House" en el aula No. 28.

La clase estará abierta de las _____ a las _____.

Me gustaría mostrarle _____

Pienso que le gustaría ver _____

Una cosa que le quisiera leer es _____

_____

Two versions of an open-house invitation—one in English and one in Spanish.

35 Holding Conferences

WHAT TEACHERS NEED TO KNOW

Conferences are designed to be a structured situation for the exchange of information and plans. They are more formal than the kinds of conversations that occur on a frequent basis between professionals and family members. Conferences should be a time during which information is exchanged freely and questions and ideas are explored. One goal of a conference should be to further develop relationships, because this is a time when relationships can grow if handled carefully.

There are many compelling reasons to hold conferences on an ongoing basis, instead of just having casual conversations with families. Casual conversations often have audiences, and they can get interrupted. Just talking regularly may keep both sides informed about aspects of learning and development on a daily or weekly basis but may not give the overall picture. A conference is the time to focus and concentrate in a private, comfortable setting. If enough time is allowed, questions and concerns can be discussed and misunderstandings cleared up. Conferences are good for providing details as well as the bigger picture of learning and development, and they have the potential to increase knowledge when mutual sharing occurs. Conferences can be the time to discuss goals and plans, as well as work to make sure that those of the program are compatible with those of the family.

Conferences should not just be held to discuss bad news and unacceptable behavior, even though the term *progress report* has just those connotations in some primary programs. Families will start dreading conferences if they don't have any positive experiences with them. Always start a conference about a child by describing the child's strengths. Then if you have a concern, be sure that you have documented the specifics and can report them objectively to the family. Listen to what the family has to say about both the strengths and the concerns. They may disagree because their experience is different from yours. That's okay.

WHAT TEACHERS CAN DO

- Recognize parents' feelings and expectations around conferences. Their own childhood experiences with schools, teachers, and grades can bring up unpleasant memories around parent–teacher conferences. Conferences can also bring up their hopes as well as fears.
- Prepare for conferences by making their purpose clear. If the purpose of the conference is to share information about a child's learning and development, plan ahead about how to do this. Have specific examples of changes in the child since the last conference. Show examples from the child's work and play (including photos or video clips when possible) as well as stories and anecdotes. Be sure you include social and emotional progress as well as physical and cognitive progress. Collect records of actual incidents that show social-emotional growth. Use storytelling to show progress.

- Conferences should be explained when the family first arrives in the program. If there is a parent handbook, it should include written material about conferences so that parents don't think something is wrong when they are asked to attend one.

- Schedule conferences so that all families can come. Timing is important. If conferences are only held during the day, some family members may be excluded. If they are only held at night, others may be excluded. Ideally, scheduling should be flexible enough that nobody is excluded.

- Open up conferences to any family member who wants to come, and watch out for thinking only of mothers when planning them. Fathers may be the most interested party, and sometimes grandparents may be as concerned with what happens at the program or school as the parents. Of course, sometimes the grandparents are raising the child, so they are taking the role of parents.

- Suggest the possibility of observation before the conference. Watching their child in action can help family members see what goes on in the program and how their child relates to others. It can also give them ideas about what to ask or comment on when they get to the conference.

- Think about ways to put family members at ease during the conference. Consider the setting and environment. Providing food or drink can help.

- Avoid using jargon. Explain in plain language what you want the parents to understand. Jargon puts you above the family and makes you an expert. You may be an expert, but so are the parents. Don't let expertise get in the way of communication or of the relationship you should be building with each family.

- Don't compare a child to other children or to charts. Be careful of saying words like *fast*, *slow*, *behind*, or *ahead*. Growing up is not a race. Be aware of which words trigger feelings. *Normal* is a trigger word, and *abnormal* is even more of one. *Typically*

Forms such as these may be used for the beginning-of-the-year conferences. Parents have the opportunity to express the dreams, wishes, and needs of their children at conferences held during the first month of school. Responsibility is shared by parent, student, and teacher.

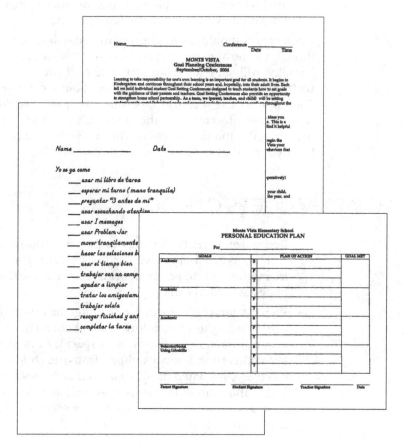

Conferences are designed to be a structured place to exchange information and make plans. They are more formal than the kinds of conversations that occur on a frequent basis between professionals and family members.

developing or *atypically developing* are better terms. Talk about *challenges* rather than *problems*. Avoid labels or judgmental words; instead, use objective ways of talking about children—describe behaviors rather than labeling them.

- Check your attitude. Make sure that you and the parent are on the same side, figuratively and literally.

- Make sure that the conversation is two-way, not just a monologue on the part of the professional.

- Know your limits. Don't assume that you can be everything to every family. Don't expect that you have the solution to every situation. Don't stretch your knowledge and experience beyond their boundaries. Sometimes you need to bring in or refer parents to other resources.

- Respect confidentiality. Gossip is unprofessional, even when it is not harmful. Don't talk about one family to another.

- Help family members to problem solve, but don't expect problems to be solved quickly or neatly. Your role is to help families sort things out if they ask you for solutions or advice. You can share your knowledge and experience, but they need to come to their own conclusions.

Make sure you and the family can understand each other. It goes without saying that you or the parent should provide an interpreter if one is needed. Don't ask the child to take that job at his own conference. Also, it's best if interpretation is done by a grown up rather than an older brother or sister of the child.

Here is an example of how a preschool teacher's careful observations gave her information to share with a child's parents in a conference. *The teacher had been watching four-year-old Kai playing by himself on the floor with blocks and small figures. She heard his voice from across the room, talking nonstop. She came over to warn him that snack time was approaching and he would need to wash his hands. She watched as he manipulated the figures, creating dramatic action while they talked loudly to each other. Kai placed two figures on top of a block tower, and one hanging down on a rope. The two on top kept looking at the dangling one, and they were having a loud argument when the teacher announced that it was snack time. Kai didn't stop playing. The teacher worked to get the other children to wash their hands and get to the snack table. When most were there, the the teacher approached Kai and insisted that he wash his hands and come to the snack table. "Awww," he protested. "Do I have to put things away?" he asked. "No, you can put a 'save sign' on what you have there," was the teacher's response. "Yeah," he said, "But I'll forget where I am." He looked forlornly at the two figures on top and the dangling one. "I'm sorry," said the teacher, "but you have to come now." Kai's face showed his distress, and he hung his head while folding his arms defiantly. Suddenly he looked up at the teacher and smiled. "I know what," he said confidently. "I'll just start a new episode." When the teacher told Kai's parents about this situation during a conference, they could see how their son was maturing. They were surprised that he used a word like episode, especially since they had no TV at home. They knew he had a great imagination—that wasn't a surprise—but this was the first time Kai's teacher had paid close attention to just how well he could play alone, and she marveled at his ability. The best thing about this story for the parents and the teacher was that it showed how Kai was making progress in coping with transitions.*

36 Considering Cross-Cultural Conferences

In cross-cultural conferences, barriers to communication may need to be considered. The first concerns concepts of time and what it means to be late. For some people, being early is important, so that when the appointed time comes, they are already there and waiting. For others, the goal is to walk in the door one minute before the scheduled time. They don't like to wait. For still others, forgivably late means five or so minutes, and some people don't consider 20 minutes after the scheduled time as truly late. Then for some people, clock time has very little meaning, and appointments may have even less. In their culture, arriving several hours or even days after the appointed time is within the bounds of courtesy.

Greetings have cultural rituals associated with them. Do you shake hands or not? What does a firm handshake mean? Does it mean you are a straightforward, competent person, or does it mean you are aggressive or rude? It depends on your culture. What does a slight touch mean in a handshake? Are you a weak person with limp hands, or are you shaking hands in the polite manner of your culture? What about eye contact? Are you respectful if you look someone in the eye, or is that disrespectful? It depends on your culture. And along with culture are gender issues. What is okay for men to do may not be okay for women, and the reverse.

If you want to be warm and friendly, do you smile and insist on being called by your first name? Do you call others by their first name? How you will be received depends on the cultural meaning others give to your warm, friendly gestures. Instead of seeing you as open and welcoming, some may feel uncomfortable or think you disrespectful.

Do you like to get right down to business once the conference begins? For some people, it's important to socialize before getting to the point of the conference. Asking personal questions about the family and each member may signal good manners for one family but feel uncomfortably intimate for another.

Of course, a huge barrier arises when families and professionals don't speak the same language. Using professional jargon creates similar problems, but that is a minor barrier compared to when there is no common language between the program and the home.

One solution to these barriers is to become an anthropologist; however, even anthropologists don't understand all the cultural differences that may emerge in one school, classroom, or family child care center.

- See yourself as a lifelong learner. Studying differences may help, but the best approach is to tune up your sensitivity. There is always more happening than appears on the surface of any interaction, even between two people of the same culture and language group. The meanings of behaviors are what is important—and are what you need to find out in order to be a good cross-cultural communicator. Observe, ask, read, listen, and discuss to find out which behaviors mean what to which people. The meanings may be cultural, but they may also be individual.

- Be prepared to make mistakes. You will make lots of them. That's the way we learn. Regard each one as a learning situation rather than as a failure on your part.

- Assume responsibility for understanding all parents by finding translators, if needed, rather than expecting parents to bring their own. Be sure the translators are competent. Also, make sure to provide all written notices in the languages of the families in your program.

- If family members speak your language somewhat, but are embarrassed about their skills, help them understand that you are in the same or even worse situation regarding their language. It's important not to assume an attitude of superiority.

- When necessary, give up your agenda, and really listen to the parent—not only the words but also the feelings behind them. Listen until the person stops talking. Don't interrupt. When it's your turn, instead of arguing, educating, or responding from your own perspective, try to state the perspective of the other person. Put the gist or spirit of what you heard into words by making a statement about the other person's feelings, experience, perceptions, beliefs, or concepts. See if you can get at the deeper message. Most people do little of this kind of listening and responding. In a conversation where there is disagreement, most people constantly push forward their own point of view. Listening skills can be learned. Best of all is the feedback you get when you've received the message that someone was trying to send, because the communication opens up and the conversation continues.

- Connect parents from the same language backgrounds so that they can help and support each other. Also, introduce them to family members from other language backgrounds. Don't let language differences keep you from inviting all parents to participate in the program at whatever level they feel comfortable with.

The following is a story about differences in concepts of time: *A visiting professor arrived to teach a class in a country where time had a very different meaning. The first day, he arrived in class a few minutes early, and only one student was there. By the time the class was supposed to start, he had only a handful of students. "They'll be here," one of the early birds assured him. The students drifted in over the first hour, and eventually, the room filled up. The professor worried that he didn't have the full time period he had prepared for. Five minutes before the end of the class, the professor expected the students to start closing their notebooks and picking up their backpacks. Five minutes later, however, when the clock indicated the end of class, not a single student had made a move to get ready to go. The class continued on for quite some time after the scheduled stopping time. The professor had a whole different sense of time to get used to.*

37 Talking with Families when Concerns Arise

WHAT TEACHERS NEED TO KNOW

Teachers and caregivers are often the first to notice that a child moves, behaves, interacts, learns, or communicates differently from other children. When you observe that you are not able to meet the child's needs, support his or her development, or foster his or her sense of belonging in the program, you may decide that the child needs more expertise than you have. That's an indication that it's time to have a meeting with the parents.

If you have a relationship with the parents and have been talking to them all along, the meeting about your concerns may not come as a surprise to them. It's quite possible that the parents, too, have been concerned and are glad to share their observations when they hear yours. Come to the meeting with notes on what you have observed and what kinds of interventions you have tried. Some suggestions for conducting the meeting are listed below.

WHAT TEACHERS CAN DO

- Before scheduling a meeting with the family to discuss the possibility of getting outside help, do a series of observations. Note specifics. Objectively and in detail, describe the behaviors that concern you. Note when and where the behaviors occurred and under what circumstances. In conjunction with your observations, see if changing the environment or your approach affects the behavior. This is important information to share with the parents. Remember, it is only appropriate for you to discuss specific behaviors that you have observed. Avoid the urge to label or diagnose.

- In the meeting, try to make the parents feel as comfortable as you can. Choose a seating arrangement that brings you together instead of separating you. Sitting behind a desk, for example, can put a psychological as well as physical barrier between you and the parents. A warmer, friendlier arrangement may work better. Provide for privacy. Set aside enough time so that the meeting isn't rushed and you can talk things through. If this is the first such meeting the parents have had, they will need to feel that you care and that they can trust you.

- Start by asking the family how they see their child, and share any positive qualities you have observed. At the outset, let the family know that you are sharing your concerns to support their child's development and to get some ideas for how to best meet their child's needs. If the family's view of the child differs from yours, be open to their perspective, ask questions, gather information, and invite them to be your partner in meeting the needs of the child.

- Before you share your concerns with them, ask if they have any concerns that they haven't already expressed. When it is time to share your concerns, be sure you communicate what you want to say clearly, without judgment, and with concrete examples. For example, rather than saying that a child is "behaving badly and bothering other children," give specifics—let the parents know that you have observed and documented that their child has a hard time sitting still and that he got up eight times while you were reading a story. Explain the behaviors that show you their child doesn't cope well with transitions. Tell about the five incidents of hitting other children during the last week. *Do not* suggest that a child has a specific diagnosis, such as attention-deficit disorder.

- If the parents don't understand your concerns, or they disagree with you, they may be upset if you suggest that a referral for further assessment is necessary. It's possible that your observations will shock or anger them. In this case, sensitively supporting the parents' feelings is called for. Just as you accept the feelings of and empathize with the child, realize that the parents need the same approach. You're not a therapist, but some of the listening skills of a therapist can serve you well. Understanding that anger or blame are common responses for people in pain helps you accept those feelings without getting defensive. The point is to focus on the feelings of the parents and listen to what they have to say without minimizing their upset or trying to talk them out of it.

- Keep clear that further assessment is a positive move and that both you and the parents have the child's best interests at heart—even if you don't see eye-to-eye at the moment.

- Sometimes the family may not choose to access resources when you first share your concerns, or they may be open to information but not ready to take action immediately. Rather than label them as being "in denial" or something else, remember that everyone moves at their own pace and accepts information differently. The family's emotional response will affect what they are able to hear and understand. Processing and integrating this information will take families varying amounts of time.

- Allow families time to accept that their child may be different from other children. That possibility is very hard for some families to hear. Unless there is a reason for urgency, let the family proceed at their own pace.

- Be prepared to support them in understanding what you have shared, repeating the information whenever necessary. Let them know that resource information is available whenever they want it. If you find that your own judgment or emotions about this interfere with your ability to respect the family as the decision maker, seek support for yourself, and don't be afraid to suggest that the family discuss this with someone else as well.

- Support the family in getting help. Let them know that you are there for them and for their child. If it comes to accessing the school district's resources or contacting an early intervention program, pediatrician, or other health care provider, let the family take the lead.

- Since many families will want to take action, be prepared to talk with them about resources for obtaining further assessment and/or possible services. This is the point at which you are "making a referral." It is generally appropriate to refer the family to their pediatrician at the same time you refer them to the local early intervention or special education resources. You should have information about services within your program, local early intervention services, special education services, and other resources.

- You cannot guarantee a family eligibility or services from another agency. You can describe what might happen after the referral and what the possible outcomes might be based on what you've learned. You can also let the family know that you are willing to provide information to the referral source. Parents must give permission for you to talk about their child with referral sources, so you will want to carefully respect the family's confidentiality and be sure that you have clear consent.

- When accessing resources, the family may face some barriers, including issues with insurance, language, cultural practices, and transportation. It's okay for you to set the process in motion for them, but rather than feeling responsible for overcoming all the barriers, focus on supporting the family, and have faith that by letting them find their own ways to meet their child's needs, you serve them and their child best (Brault, 2007).

38 Helping the Child Enter the School or Program

Preparations for the first day should start ahead of time when the child will be starting school or entering an early care and education program for the first time. It's better when parents help their child get used to separation or a new situation in small doses. Often the children who have the most trouble separating upon entering a kindergarten, new school, or other early childhood program are those who are away from family for the first time, although that is not always true. Ideally, the child also has some familiarity with the teacher or caregiver before the first day. Those programs that are fully dedicated to partnering with parents sometimes figure out how to make home visits to the family before the start of the program. This not only lets them meet the family on its home territory, but also the child who is being enrolled. Another option is to invite the child and family to visit ahead of time so that the child can meet the teacher or caregiver and become familiar with the setting. Either of those approaches ensures that the child doesn't begin the first day in a strange place with a strange adult.

A parent handbook can help the family feel more secure about entering a new program. Information is always helpful! Of course, if the handbook is only in English, and some families don't speak or read English, it won't be very helpful. There should be translations into all the languages represented among the entering families.

In child care programs there is no first day of the new school year. Child care is available year round, and children can come and go at any time. There is no particular period when a whole group of families would enroll at the same time. In school programs, however, there is a first day of school. Here are some ideas about how to create a more gentle beginning for families and children at the beginning of the school year.

Consider staggering family visits to the school before the first day. Arrange a few at a time so families and children can get to know each other without being overwhelmed by a crowd. Also stagger starting days so that just a few children come at a time. If possible, having shorter days the first week can help children get used to school gradually. In most public schools this is difficult because the school loses money, but in private programs and seasonal preschools it is sometimes possible to have a gentle beginning and lessen separation issues.

Some programs invite families to help their child enter the program for the first time by staying until the child is comfortable. This kind of invitation sets a warm tone and gives messages to both the child and the family member that this is their place and they are welcome. This first experience can encourage parents to get involved in the program. Although some early childhood professionals would prefer that parents drop off their children and leave right away, there are some advantages in letting those parents who can and want to stay, do so. However, some families may come from a background where home and school are completely separate and they see no reason to step inside the classroom or get involved in anyway, including helping their child separate.

A common situation is for a parent to want to sneak out without saying good-bye because she knows her child will cling and cry. It is better to discuss this possibility ahead of time rather than waiting until it happens. The early childhood professional can show empathy for a parent who has feelings about her child's separation behaviors. At the same time, this professional can help the parent understand that it is harder on the child when they come to distrust the parent than it is to express their feelings about separation openly.

Of course, when a child has been in early care and education programs from a young age, he may be used to separation. Nevertheless, the first day of kindergarten or first grade may be a bigger transition than he is used to. It may be a new setting with new regulations. The group's size may be larger, and having parents in the classroom on the first day isn't as feasible as in programs for younger children.

WHAT TEACHERS CAN DO

- Make everybody feel welcome—children and family members alike. Respond to the diversity in the group in ways that say, "Welcome everybody; you are all accepted." This could include using some words of their language, or having pictures on the wall, books around the room and music playing that reflect the cultures of the group.

- Reassure families that their children are in good hands.

- Demonstrate acceptance of any upset feelings—both the child's and the parent's. It helps if they can both see that their feelings don't upset you, too.

- Help parents understand that their child's separation anxiety is quite common and nothing to worry about. Indeed, it shows attachment, and that's a good thing. Some parents may view protests that are an expression of separation anxiety as bad manners. Assure them that you don't see it that way.

- If the parent is allowed to and chooses to stay in the classroom to help the child separate gently, suggest that the parent let the child decide when the parent can leave. Although this doesn't always work, it gives the child a sense of self-confidence when it does.

- Pair a new child with another child. Pair the parent with another, more experienced parent.

- Put up a picture board and post the child's picture with his or her family. You might also include the teacher and his or her family. In a program with other staff members besides the teacher, including their pictures also may help the children and families feel at home.

- Allow "transition objects"—something special brought from home that can comfort the child when separation issues get her down.

Good-byes the first day can be hard. Accept the child's feelings, and try pairing him up with another child.

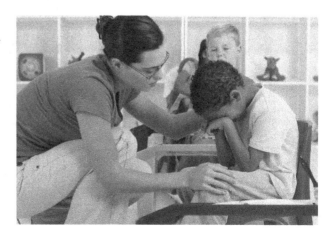

Here's a story about how a child figured out on his own how to be brave when starting kindergarten: *Nicky was born prematurely, got a rocky start in life, and was medically fragile for the first two years of his life. He had experience in two different early care and education settings before starting kindergarten. Each time he began a new program, his parent remained until he was comfortable staying by himself. Kindergarten was a big step after preschool, though, and Nicky started worrying. Before school started, he attended a parent meeting with his mother. When the teacher announced that the children would stay in the classroom with the aide while the parents took a tour of the school grounds, Nicky grabbed his mother's hand and wouldn't let go. He was the only child that day who got the school grounds tour with the parents. When the meeting was over, the mother told the teacher that she always stayed in school with Nicky until he felt comfortable when entering a new program. The teacher was very clear and said in a firm voice, "No parents in the classroom the first day." Both Nicky and his mother were worried about the first day. They had a talk. His mother explained that this new school had new rules, and even though neither of them liked the one about no parents in the classroom, that's just the way it was. "So what are you going to do?" she asked him. He thought about it for a while and then said, "I'll go under the table." Once he had a strategy, he felt a lot braver. The first day came, and he let go of his mother's hand and walked straight into the classroom. After the session, she picked him up and was glad to see a big smile on his face. "How did it go?" she asked. "Well," he said, "I did just what I said. I went under the table. Then a girl said, 'Teacher, there's a boy under the table.' So I came out." That's all he ever said about it, but apparently the strategy worked! The second day, he came up with a new strategy. He wore his Superman tee shirt.*

In the "Daily Guidelines" section in this parent handbook, there are some ideas and specific instructions under a subsection called "Bringing Your Child."

DAILY GUIDELINES

→ **Bringing Your Child**

It is important to help your child make the transition from home to school. If a staff member has not greeted your child, take your child to one of the teachers. State licensing requires that teachers greet children and their parents and assess the health of the child before the parent leaves.

A few things to remember:

1. You may bring your child ten minutes before the block begins. This gives some time for greeting the teacher, looking around the school with your child, and walking to your class.

2. Sign your child in on the daily sign-in sheet when you arrive. You must use a complete signature.

3. Pin your child's nametag on and assist in hanging up his or her coat.

4. Let teachers know any information that will help them as they work with your child (lack of sleep, change in daily schedule, new medicine, et cetera).

Leaving with Your Child

1. Sign your child out when you pick him/her up. Only persons listed on the Emergency Card may pick up a child. The parent of record must inform the staff verbally and give written permission if someone else is picking-up the child. The person picking-up must check-in with the Children's Center Office and present photo identification before the child can be released.

2. Leave your child's nametag in the place designated by your child's teacher.

3. Check your child's cubby for treasures waiting to go home.

4. Take home wet clothes.

5. If your child has worn DVC extra clothing home, please clean and return it the next day you attend school.

6. CHECK YOUR PARENT MAILBOX. PLEASE READ AND RESPOND TO ANY MEMOS OR NOTICES.

39 Maintaining Home Language

There are many misconceptions about children who arrive in school or other early childhood programs with a home language that is different from English. Because these children may be perceived as language deficient or potential candidates for having a language delay, it is important that everyone recognizes and appreciates the development these children have made in their own language, regardless of their current proficiency in English. The benefits of preserving home language, and encouraging the child's continued development in it, are many. Adding English to what they already know encourages bilingualism, which is a worthy goal for a number of reasons (Charmian, 2007). It's important for teachers not to consider bilingualism as a problem but rather as a blessing.

Language and culture are vitally linked. Families use language to pass on their culture to their children and teach them how to grow up and remain members of the particular group or groups to which the family belongs. Thus, language also plays an important role in identity formation. One big issue for children growing up is discovering where they belong. Those children who lose their home language also lose important connections to their family and their people.

Neither language nor culture is taught in formal lessons. Rather, both are learned during interactions through which children read the expectations of those around them. Some of these informal "lessons" related to culture may be embedded in language, and some not.

What is a child's *home language*? Home language can be broadly or narrowly defined. A narrow way of looking at home language is whether dictionaries and grammar books exist to give the language standards. A more useful way for early childhood educators to look at home language is as the language that is spoken in the child's home.

When the great "Ebonics debate" arose in California a few years ago, it was argued across the United States whether teachers should accept the way some African American children speak if those children are speaking what has been called Ebonics. Certainly, it may feel different to support a child when the family speaks Standard English (or, as it is sometimes called, *Status English*) from supporting an Ebonics-speaking child. Or consider two families that both speak Spanish. One speaks Standard Spanish, and the other speaks what some label as "Spanglish." Both Ebonics and the dialects used by some children from Spanish-speaking backgrounds are regarded as inferior by some who speak Standard English or Standard Spanish. But it's important to remember that when it comes to language, culture, family ties and issues of identity, acceptance of the family and their language, whatever it is, makes a difference to the child's self-esteem, which can support learning and development.

When teachers disapprove of the home language, some children pick up messages, spoken or not, that cause them to give up their home language in favor of English. That's a subtractive approach to English language learning. An additive approach is much better. When children learn Standard English as well as continue to develop in their home language, they become bilingual, which is a decided advantage to the child, the family, the community, and the nation. Bilinguals feel at home with their family and also out in the English-speaking world.

Nobody is asking teachers to learn to speak all the languages that may show up in their classrooms. Of course, they aren't going to be required to learn what they may consider a substandard dialect, but there are compelling reasons not to look down on children whose families speak such a dialect. There are also compelling reasons to bring family or community members into the classroom or program if the school or program has no other adults who speak the language of the family.

Of course, all children in the United States must eventually learn to speak English and to use it in powerful ways. Maintaining home language is a way to support English language learners. If done well, the child can end up bilingual and bicultural, which would be a great educational goal for *all* children in this country—including those from families whose home language is English.

WHAT TEACHERS CAN DO

- Encourage families to work with you to maintain the home language with their children. Share with those families the fact that in this country, historically, the average immigrant family faced the loss of their home language in three generations. Today, it's often only one generation, as children begin to feel ashamed and sometimes make the decision on their own to turn their backs on their parents' and grandparents' language.

- Understand that some families and communities struggle to maintain their home language. Find them and support them in that struggle. Get them together with families that are so concerned with their children learning English that they don't face up to the risk of the children losing their home language. If the latter families hear stories of adults who found they couldn't go home and feel like they belong there once they lost the language of their family, or stories about discipline problems when children and adults no longer share the same language, they may be motivated to work with you to maintain the home language in their children.

- Consider children's emotional state as they are acquiring English, and make their emotional well-being a primary goal.

- Find ways to bring each child's home language into the classroom or center. Children's emotional well-being can be supported by hearing their own language when not at home. Getting families involved can help. Volunteers can also help. Community centers, social groups, and religious groups can be sources of volunteers for the classroom or center.

- Look for books and other written materials in the children's home language. Bring in other media from their culture as well, such as recorded music. Live music is even better. Be sure the environment reflects the language and culture of every family in the classroom or center.

- Language, learning, and thinking are tied together. Encourage children to use their strongest language to help them think through something or solve a problem.

- Become an advocate for bilingualism, and work with others to change unfair English-only assessment practices.

- Be careful to avoid mislabeling those learning English as having disabilities or language delays.

- Don't be fooled by the myth that children pick up a second language in no time at all. It takes years to develop to full academic competence in one's own language; thus, English learners may pick up conversational abilities, but acquiring the full range of linguistic competence in English won't happen any more rapidly than language acquisition in monolingual English-speaking children. And of course, if children continue to develop those competencies in their home language, and learn English competencies as well, they will eventually become truly bilingual.

- Find resources and support for yourself to do what can be a hard job. Nobody ever said teaching was easy—rewarding, yes, but easy, no!

40 Easing Children Through Transitions

WHAT TEACHERS NEED TO KNOW

One of the hardest parts of parenting is keeping up with children moving from one stage of development to another. The most dramatic moves come in the first two years, but moving from one stage to the next is a continual process throughout childhood and, indeed, throughout life. Behaviors change as children move to the next stage, and families may see these new behaviors as problems rather than as an indication of greater maturity. Here's where effective parenting education can come in handy. Families can learn new approaches they can take for each new stage. Most families haven't taken child development courses, so that's a perfect topic for parenting education for families that find it helpful. Articles to read, discussion groups, even lectures and videos are often gratefully received by families that are facing a new stage with which they aren't familiar. Of course all these materials (and lectures) need to be in the language of the families!

Moving from stage to stage is one kind of transition. Moving from one classroom to another, or from one program to another, is another transition that sometimes coincides with a developmental change, and sometimes not. In a program that tries hard to be developmentally appropriate, very young children may face many transitions if each new stage means a new classroom with a new teacher. When you consider the issue of relationships—child relating to teacher or caregiver, as well as parents relating to new adults, at each developmental stage—the constant transitioning can be very unsettling. A technique called *looping*, where the teacher stays with the class or group for several years, is one answer to the problem of continually severed relationships. But no matter what, there always comes a time when children and their parents have to move on.

The daily routine in any program also is full of transitions. In the primary grades there may be transitions between group instruction and individual seat work, but the main transitions come at recess and lunch. Those are breaks and are usually welcomed by most children. The end of recess may be a major transition for some children, who may resist it. For programs with younger children the transitions come regularly between activities, and typically include arrival, free play, cleanup, outdoor time, hand washing, group time, snack time, a repeat of the routine of the first part of the morning, which leads to lunch in full-day programs, followed by nap, and so forth, ending in "good-bye time."

Other transitions that can affect children come from living in a constantly changing family. Some families' lives are disrupted on a regular basis. There isn't much a teacher can do about this except to understand the behaviors that might show up in a child in this situation.

What follows are strategies for helping teachers deal with all kinds of transitions, including during the daily routine. There are also tips for how families can help their children to make transitions, whether from one stage to another, one room to another, or one program to another, especially in a constantly changing family.

WHAT TEACHERS CAN DO

- In the classroom, create a predictable and visible routine, using various means to signal the end of one activity or period and the beginning of another. Give children warnings before each change and, depending on their age, tell them how soon the change will occur. If transitions present more problems than are tolerable, consider reducing the number of them in the daily routine.

- Helping a child (and family) transition from one classroom to another, or from one program to another, may be out of your hands except to prepare the family and child before the time comes. If the child is moving to a new classroom in the same program you can give plenty of warning ahead of time so the child isn't surprised by the change. If the whole group is moving, that's different. If the child is able to visit the new classroom before the move, it may be helpful. Sometimes it's possible to transition the child gradually when the new classroom is in the same location.

- Take your position as a parenting educator seriously. Just as you respond to the care and education of children as individuals, so should you respond to family members as individuals. Some family members are new at parenting, not having been around children before. They are most likely eager to know more, especially if they perceive you as a resource and not a threat—as someone who can give them ideas, but who will not criticize them. Other families may be much more experienced at parenting. They can be resources to families that need skills, information, and support.

- There are many ways to assist learning about parenting, including about how to facilitate smooth transitions. Just as early childhood professionals pay attention to the different learning styles of children, so they should pay attention to those of parents and other family members. What works best? It could be articles tucked into the parent's mailbox in response to questions asked; discussions around a topic that a parent or group of parents shows interest in; a lending library with a variety of materials on subjects related to parenting; a list of suggested readings; observations followed by discussion; videos; suggested websites; and pairing experienced parents with inexperienced ones. These are just a few ideas for how to match teaching approaches and resources to individual learning styles.

- Transitions that are not related to developmental stages should be gradual and infrequent. Some children suffer even with small transitions, such as from one activity to another. They resist even little changes. They don't like new things. Other children are less reluctant, but transitions create some stress in almost all children

- Remember that with every transition children make, the family is also affected. Moving on is felt by everybody.

- Some child care programs lack continuity of care. Staff members keep changing and the child never gets to know any one adult very well or for very long. If you see a child who seems to be suffering from that situation, and if it's appropriate, you might mention to the family the advantage of a family child care home as an early care and education setting. A child who changes to family day care may find it a real contrast from the previous number of transitions and lack of stability. Some family child care providers have several children from the same family and may stay connected with the family for years. Children often come into a family

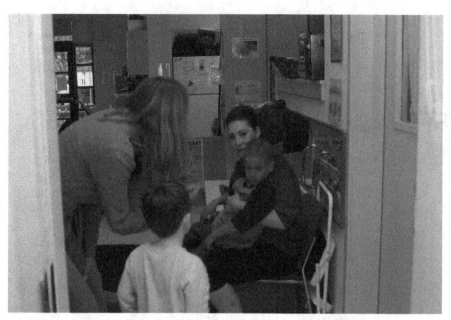

This child is experiencing a transition and needs a little help from adults.

child care home as newborns and may stay there until they outgrow early care and education. In some cases, the child grows up, has children of his own, and sends those children to the same provider he went to in his early years. Talk about long-term relationships and continuity of care!

- When children live in families that constantly change in composition, there isn't much a teacher or other early childhood educator can do except offer support. For example, grandparents may temporarily take the place of parents in the military who are deployed. This can also occur in single parent families when the parent is unavailable to parent, or when the parent has a substance abuse problem, or is incarcerated. Some children live in two homes and move back and forth between parents. Children of immigrant parents who have no papers can be left behind in the home of a relative or friend when the parents are caught up in a "sweep" and incarcerated or deported. In all these cases, support for both the child and whoever is parenting the child can be invaluable!

Here is an example of what happened when an infant–toddler program decided to institute a continuity-of-care system where babies stayed with the same caregivers until they were old enough to move to preschool. *The caregivers stayed with the group even though the environment changed as the babies outgrew the room they started out in. The first time around, nobody knew exactly how this would work, and some were doubtful that it would. There was some resistance on the part of the caregivers because they were used to a certain age group and didn't think they would like working with older children. But that turned out not to be a problem once they got connected to the babies. They really enjoyed "moving up with them" and seeing more of the developmental sequence unfold. By the time the first group was almost old enough to transition to preschool, which was in the same building, and leave the infant–toddler staff behind, there was some concern about the separation process. After being with the same caregiver for so long, wouldn't they suffer when they said good-bye? The surprise was that the children did great. They were excited about becoming preschoolers, and the transition was gradual enough that they got used to the preschool room and teachers before the final move came. The new world and people in it were so interesting and exciting to them that the separation was a gentle one. Even the caregivers found letting go easy because they felt the children were ready to move on and they knew they would continue to see them. They just wouldn't be their caregivers anymore. The other surprise was that the group who suffered separation anxieties was the parents! They worried about the new teacher and program. They didn't want to let go of the people they had grown to know and trust.*

41 Bringing Nature into Children's Lives

WHAT TEACHERS NEED TO KNOW

With childhood obesity rates rising, it becomes clearer and clearer that something is wrong with the lifestyle of many American children. It's easy to see the roots of this problem when you look to the beginning of life for the average American baby. Strapped into various devices which reduce their ability to exercise, babies spend most of their waking and all of their sleeping hours indoors. They are set up for a sedentary, indoor lifestyle.

Comparing the average American baby's life and health with the babies studied for more than 60 years in a residential nursery in Budapest, Hungary, you see quite a contrast. The nursery, called the Pikler Institute after its founder, Dr. Emmi Pikler, brought science together with some old-fashioned ideas about fresh air, exercise, and freedom to explore both in and out of doors. Babies and young children in the Institute not only play outdoors every day except in the most extreme weather, they also nap outside—from birth on (Gonzalez-Mena, 2004).

Part of this old-fashioned idea is that children should be free to move and explore, which at the Pikler Institute they learn starting in infancy. Instead of being strapped into baby carriers, swings, and strollers or being sat up in high chairs, the babies at the Pikler Institute move naturally, unencumbered by modern baby equipment. As a result, they gain movement skills, balance, and above all, motivation to learn. They grow into active preschoolers who see themselves as competent learners who don't need adults gushing over them, praising every little thing they accomplish or offering rewards for learning. They are natural learners, eager to discover, find out how things work, and gain knowledge of everything around them and beyond.

Put children who have that kind of early education into a classroom where they are required to sit and memorize disembodied facts or repeat answers to questions on flash cards for long periods and you can see that either they will cause problems or they will come to take on a less active lifestyle. That inactive lifestyle is definitely a trend, as outside pressures make teachers teach in ways they may not agree with. Added to this is the fact that in some schools recess is an endangered species because it is thought to cut into learning time.

Richard Louv (2008a, b) is trying hard to reverse one of these trends, which he calls the *denatured childhood*. He is a champion for exploration and free play in natural surroundings, which some children never have a chance to do. He cites studies that show that time spent indoors in front of a television or computer is related to growing obesity in children (and in adults).

Free, unstructured play is important to children's mental, physical, and emotional health. Free play that takes place in natural surroundings increases cognitive flexibility, emotional capacity, critical thinking, problem solving, creative use of imagination,

This child is experiencing nature and learning about math at the same time.

These children are learning about nature through exploring together in a natural setting. Of course, an adult is there with them.

self-esteem, and self-discipline. It makes children smarter, more cooperative, more energetic, happier, and healthier. Playing in natural settings is valuable because nature is a highly complex system and is a lot bigger than all of us. Children can find more to do in natural settings than in most other settings because nature has a good many of what play theorists call *loose parts*. "In any environment, both the degree of inventiveness and creativity, and the possibility of discovery, are directly proportional to the number and kind of variables in it" (Simon Nicholson, quoted in Gies, 2008, p. 26).

Spending time in a natural environment encourages children to take reasonable risks, which is an important part of growing up. The child who has been raised in a risk-free environment and/or under adult control at all times has little experience judging which risks he or she can handle and are worth taking. Learning what one is physically capable of is an essential childhood task, and it is learned in environments where there are opportunities for taking reasonable risks. According to Gies (2008), a study at the University of Illinois found that contact with nature, and the risk-taking it involves, can even reduce attention-deficit disorder.

WHAT TEACHERS CAN DO

- Observe your daily schedule and calculate the amount of time children spend in free and unstructured play that is not part of an adult-directed game or activity. If constraints work against expanding free play, or if there is no chance at all for free play during the school day, get together with the parents and figure out how to expand that time outside of school, especially if it tends to be limited there also.

- Be prepared for some parents to protest some of the ideas presented here for several reasons. Most preschool teachers who have been in the field for some time know that some families see free play as a waste of time when children need to get ready for kindergarten. They may prefer structured learning activities. Furthermore, the messy play activities that are regarded as important for sensory exploration can cause parental consternation. Also, getting out and into nature, as in the suggestions that follow, may not be a part of a family's cultural tradition. It might be an economic issue for families in low income neighborhoods if nature isn't easily available without transportation. Don't give up; just understand that the path to nature may not be an easy one for some families.

- Become more aware of nature-deficit disorder, and together with the parents, figure out what to do about it. A good start would be to get back to nature yourself (if you need to) and so provide a model for the parents and children alike. Your enthusiasm can be contagious.

- Bring nature into the classroom in ways that children can get involved with in a hands-on way. See if you can find some parents to partner with you in this attempt.

- Become an advocate for stopping the de-naturizing of your community and for restoring nature where possible. Some forward-looking schools are tearing up sections of asphalt in the playground and planting gardens.

- Become an advocate (and bring parents along with you) for putting nature study into the curriculum if it is not already there. Teach natural history in developmentally appropriate ways, depending on the age of the child.

- If possible, take field trips into natural environments. Get parents involved. This may be difficult, but it's worth a try.

42 Addressing Obesity with Nutrition

WHAT TEACHERS NEED TO KNOW

More American children are overweight than ever before. Why? One reason is lack of exercise. Another is an unhealthy diet. According to Michael Pollan, in his book *In Defense of Food* (2008), most Americans' diet consists of highly processed, food-like products, rather than real food. Those products contain vast amounts of refined wheat, sugars, and corn syrups—even those that don't taste sweet. Though vitamins and minerals are added, the end product is still far less nutritious than the original, unprocessed food substance. Meat is full of hormones designed to make animals fat and tasty, but when people eat meat, and those same hormones go into their bodies, it may be adding to their weight problems.

One mother with a girl in child care complained to the teachers and directors about the daily menu, which she felt was sadly lacking in proper nutrition. But because the program depended on government funding and therefore had to follow government guidelines, they couldn't do much to change things. Here's where advocacy can help—though the food lobbies in Washington that want to keep the status quo are powerful.

There are huge obstacles to proper nutrition for young children. For one thing, families in low income brackets may have difficulty getting all the healthy ingredients they and their children need using food stamps and food pantries. An important consideration for low income families is getting enough food to fill up their children's stomachs. One teacher of teachers sends her students out to purchase food for a family of four with the dollar allotment provided for food stamps in her state. They are required to make it all healthy. Most find it nearly impossible to follow nutrition guidelines and still fill up four stomachs. Part of the solution is education about how to create delicious, nutritious, and filling foods with inexpensive, natural ingredients. Another part is needing to change acquired tastes, many of which come from advertisements in the media. It's a very complex issue to get healthy food into children.

By the time children get to kindergarten and the early grades, their food tastes and what they are accustomed to are pretty well set. That's why parental involvement and education are so important in the early years. If teachers and parents get together and explore nutritious food choices, each can learn from the other. Cultural differences may be great, but that can be an advantage if families are still eating the diets of their ancestors. It seems that the simple, natural diets of yesteryear were much healthier—without all the additives and innovations of modern food processing. But of course, there are lots of pressures to adopt the common diets of today, which include a heavy dose of fast food eaten in cars and on the run, as well as prepared food, whether frozen in ready-to-heat containers or in boxes off the grocery store shelves.

Whoever packed this lunch box seems to know about the health benefits of fresh fruit.

WHAT TEACHERS CAN DO

- Help parents understand the value of fresh food over processed food products, and work to provide more fresh food if you or the program is responsible for what the children eat while away from home.

- Set examples of healthy eating habits. Look for nutritious snacks to serve at parent meetings. Get parents to contribute ideas and food.

- Create a series of parenting meetings focused on nutrition education by bring in cooking experts to demonstrate how to make delicious food out of inexpensive, healthy ingredients. Or bring in parents to demonstrate healthy food preparation based on family recipes. This can be a great chance to experience diversity. Get the children involved too. One idea is to collect family recipes and have the children help create cookbooks. The final book then includes the children's words as well as the family's recipe.

- Have meetings to exchange ideas with families on nutritional issues.

- Grow food, if possible, and involve the children. There's nothing like pulling out a carrot you helped grow and eating it for snack. Make parents part of your gardening activity, and encourage them to take the idea home and try it themselves.

- Get children into small groups to cook in class, if possible. Involve parents in this classroom activity so that they can do the same at home. A number of academic lessons can come out of one cooking activity. Early literacy is one lesson when you use individual recipe cards. If the children are old enough to read, the cards can contain words. If you're working with younger children, pictures will work—and the children are still getting "reading lessons" when they see a series of picture symbols and find the meaning in them. Children get math lessons as they measure ingredients—two tablespoons of this and half a teaspoon of that. And if children are working in groups, it also becomes a socialization activity.

Here is an example of what one director did about working with parents around nutrition: *The director of a child care program who worked with low-income parents decided to have a series of parent meetings around nutritional issues. She brought in an expert chef who did cooking demonstrations, after which the parents in attendance ate the delicious dishes they had learned to prepare. The chef introduced ingredients that were highly nutritious, inexpensive, and easy to come by, but not well known to the families. These new dishes caught on, and the parents loved the cooking lessons. Quite a different approach than giving a lecture on nutrition and making parents feel guilty about what they were feeding their children!*

43 Dealing with Media Issues

....

WHAT TEACHERS NEED TO KNOW

The electronic media—including television, computers, electronic games and toys, and personal devices such as smart phones and tablets—have raised health concerns about the sedentary lifestyle they promote. Another health concern is that commercials in the media contribute to the formation of unhealthy eating habits. Television commercials used to be the main concern, but now commercials are everywhere you turn, and they can influence adults and children alike to consume excess calories. Eating non-nutritious meals and snacks can be strongly influenced by peer modeling as well as advertising. The effects on young children from watching violence on television and in computer games is another negative health concern with electronic media. And electronic bullying is an issue getting much attention nowadays, although it is more common with children older than the early childhood category.

Fortunately, we now have research that can inform families and teachers about early exposure to electronic media. Videos designed for babies were once advertised as ways to "make babies smarter" and were named after a well-known genius. Research done at the University of Washington compared babies who watched those videos with babies who didn't watch them or any other television designed for babies. They discovered that the video watchers actually had fewer vocabulary words when compared to the non-watchers!

Jane Healy, an educational psychologist and author of books about early childhood learning, is a strong advocate for helping teachers and parents take a good look at the time young children spend with screens instead of out in the real, physical world. We don't need research to tell us that addiction to screens is widespread—and growing—across the whole age range. We can see it everywhere we go. Most of us can probably sense it in our families and in ourselves.

These addictions can start in infancy as babies are propped up in front of the television screen to watch programs with images and sounds designed especially for them—or just any old program that the rest of the family is watching. Also some parents and teachers are anxious to prepare children for the future by getting them started early on computers. The main concern here is what young children are missing out on by spending a lot of time looking at or interacting with screens. They are missing what earlier generations did in childhood during their free time—running around outdoors and playing with other children, often in natural surroundings.

Nobody ever proved that children have to be sitting down to learn. Young children are active learners, and they need plenty of chances to move, explore, and play freely, which they may not be getting at home. They also need concrete experiences as part of their learning. Because of using screens as both entertainment and learning tools, children today are doing much more sitting and watching than any generation in history. No wonder obesity is a growing problem.

According to Healy (2008), "Time spent with computers in the early years not only subtracts from important developmental tasks but may also entrench bad learning habits, leading to poor motivation and even symptoms of learning disability" (p. 75).

That's a strong statement! And that was 2008. Now the electronic media has expanded well beyond computers; just watch any place where people are waiting—the airport, bus stop, doctor's office. People sitting at tables in restaurants waiting for their food may well be looking at their phones—not just to make calls, but using other features. Whatever they are doing, they aren't talking to each other! Most people in public, including children, have some kind of electronic device in their hands. And if young children don't have their own, adults are sharing theirs so children can look at pictures, play games, watch videos, and so forth.

But computers in early care and education programs are still an issue. No one has shown that computers in preschool contribute to children's learning, development, health, or well-being, though computers and software are being developed and marketed to families with young children and to early childhood teachers. It's up to families and teachers to be wise about what they buy for children.

Learning in the early years should take place in a physical and social context, not coming through disembodied screens. Children learn best when they have personal interactions with adults and other children. As Healy (2008) puts it, "The brain does its important work in a context of relaxed exploration guided primarily by the child and supported by helpful and emotionally responsive but not overly intrusive adults" (p. 76).

In such situations, children are also learning to focus their attention instead of flitting from one thing to another. Electronic media, with their bells and whistles, pop-ups, graphics, and other distractions, work against a steady stream of attention.

Along with other early childhood experts, Healy sees age seven as the appropriate time to begin using computers to help children learn. She says that computer learning for young children, even those at age seven, should be backed up with manipulative activities away from the screen. For many educators and psychologists, age seven is a developmental milestone—children are getting their second set of teeth, and their brains are less tied to the here and now of the concrete world. However, they still learn concretely; thus, manipulative materials that they can touch, hold, and move around are still important.

Plenty has been written about young children viewing violent programming, and the danger of commercials turning even toddlers into consumers. Parents should be involved in discussions about the effects of the amount of violence children are seeing on screens at home, and they should do what they can to eliminate or at least minimize it. That's where parents as advocates can make a difference in what is shown during prime time, when children have easy access to such media.

Children's experiences in natural settings are greatly reduced when they spend a lot of time in front of screens. It doesn't work to just show them nature programs as a substitute. There are no fresh air, exercise, or sensory experiences when watching nature programs. Furthermore, these programs set up expectations so that when children do get outdoors to experience nature they expect to see things happen like they do on television—birds hatching from eggs or bull moose fighting. With those kinds of expectations, children may find being out in nature boring because things don't happen as fast as on screens. It takes patience and observation skills to study nature; watching films doesn't necessarily promote those skills (except in the photographers who make the movies).

WHAT TEACHERS CAN DO

- Work with families in partnership around issues of concern related to media. Find out if they have any concerns.
- See if any families you work with are worried about the amount of time their children spend in front of the TV. Ask about the images they want their children to see and not see.

Addiction to television can start in infancy and continue into the adult years.

- If you are working with infants and toddlers, find out what the families believe about TV and other screen devices for that age group.

- If appropriate, plan a parent meeting or a series of meetings centered around the subject of media. Infant–toddler teachers could focus on TV for babies. Preschool and primary teachers could broaden the discussion to media in general.

- One parent meeting could focus on violence in the media. What do families think about media exposing children to violence, not just through shows, but also through the news and games? You may want to examine your own attitudes as well. This could lead to a rich discussion as everybody learns about perspectives that are different from their own.

- As children grow older, bullying in social media becomes a concern. Younger children may have already heard news reports of suicides as a result of "cyber-bullying." Is that a concern for families in your program? Would parents like ideas about how to address this issue?

- Help parents identify what is positive and what is not when it comes to media. If appropriate, share your ideas about how to help children live a healthier lifestyle by monitoring their use of electronic media and endeavoring to reduce the negative effects that come from overusing some kinds of media.

- If you aren't now using computers with children but are being pressured to do so, help those who are applying the pressure to understand that starting children too early can create bigger problems than starting them too late.

- Do make some important decisions before you go into computers. Don't spend money on computers unless you already have all the developmentally appropriate materials you need. Don't skimp on those to get computers.

- If you already have or are going to get computers, set them up so that their use is a social experience. Let children work together and talk while they are working.

- Prepare yourself by observing how children use computers, and if you see problems, start thinking about how to solve them.

- Get training in using computers with young children.

- Research and make sure you are buying developmentally appropriate software.

- Be clear about what you want children to learn from the computer, and look for software that accomplishes your goal. Don't be dazzled by programs that don't do what you want.

- Monitor the amount of "screen time" children receive in your program. Be sure they also get plenty of hands-on experiences and regular outdoor exercise. Share your concerns about screen time with parents, if appropriate.

- If you are using DVDs or television, make sure what you show is developmentally appropriate. Eliminate commercials if you can. Limit the time children spend sitting and watching. Be sure you have plenty of active and interactive learning experiences going on.

- Discuss issues around electronic media with parents and other family members. Share ideas. Discuss how to solve the problems that can arise.

- Become aware of advocacy groups that have children's interests in mind when it comes to media content, including commercials. Share this information with families if appropriate.

44 Maintaining Stability During Divorce

WHAT TEACHERS NEED TO KNOW

Special attention is needed for children and families who are going through a divorce. It is a major transition for all the family members and may involve angry feelings and inappropriate behavior by the two people getting divorced. A breakup often involves financial stress as well as a move from the original residence. A lower standard of living for the children may result. The original family no longer exists in the same way. This may bring feelings of loss, because one parent is no longer as much a part of the children's lives. Sometimes the siblings are split up. There may be a long, unsettled period in which life is not predictable and a sense of security is disrupted. This rocky period usually starts before the actual divorce, as parents go through a period of conflict that can be brief or long and drawn out.

WHAT TEACHERS CAN DO

- Though you can't do anything about the tensions being felt at home, you can help parents deal with their children's feelings and resulting behaviors, which may include fears, sleep disturbance, fussing, and whining. Sometimes children regress—go back to an earlier stage of life and pick up old behaviors that they had shed long ago, such as bed-wetting or thumb-sucking. A child who is ordinarily easy to get along with may become demanding, defiant, or disobedient. The usually secure child may become dependent and show separation anxiety. In recess or playtime, you may notice less positive interaction, more aggression, and perhaps less involvement as the usually active child becomes more of an observer. Older children may look sad, have difficulty focusing, and show fear, anxiety, or anger.

- Sometimes children may conclude that the divorce was their fault. It's important they understand that this is not true and that they are not to blame.

- Of course, parents have their own feelings, and although you are not a therapist you can offer them support. You may not be able to meet their needs, but you can listen to them if they feel like talking. On the other hand, they may not feel like talking. They may be so upset that they turn away and become less interactive with the teacher or caregiver. Understanding and empathy are the best response to changes in parental attitudes and behavior during this difficult period.

- Community resources are available for families in stress. Know what they are, and make information available to the parents. You can't be all things to all people, but you can point family members toward counseling resources. And Parents Without Partners, a self-help group, can be a support for them. Have contact information available.

- Make available books about divorce—for both children and adults.

You can't be all things to all people, but you can support families going through a divorce and point them toward appropriate community resources.

- Be very clear about who is authorized to pick up the children, and who is not.
- Know that this period will pass. Be kind, gentle, and understanding.
- Examine your own attitudes and feelings about divorce. Become aware of any stereotypes you have about families who are undergoing this transition or about the consequences for children. It is different for each family and for each person in the family. The process of divorce may make for difficult times and correspondingly difficult behavior, but don't decide that you already know the long-term effects on the children. Many of the ideas about negative outcomes do not hold true. Children are not necessarily worse off because of their parents' divorce, nor are they necessarily worse off living in single-parent families. There are many myths and misconceptions about children of divorced parents. If parents are miserable together, it most likely has a negative effect on the children; this may be alleviated once the split comes.

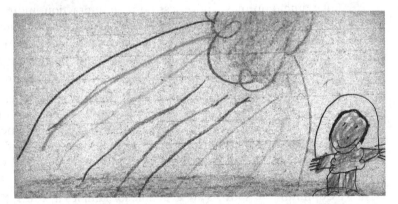

Even a divorce can have some light spots. This child may be indicating that rain can result in rainbows.

45 Coping with a Death in the Family

WHAT TEACHERS NEED TO KNOW

A death in the family can be a traumatic event for everybody—especially for a child. The death of the parent who is the main caregiver can be devastating because not only is there a sense of loss but also tremendous feelings of insecurity as the child asks, consciously or unconsciously, "Who will take care of me now?" Death can shake a child to the core and affect his or her development and sense of self. A good deal of support is needed—both for the child and family members. Teachers aren't therapists, but there are some things they can do to help the child and family through what is bound to be a difficult period.

Many factors enter into how a death affects a child. A slow death, with the child supported through the dying process, is very different from a sudden and violent death, and both can be different from a soldier dying overseas in the service of his or her country. Of course, any death in the family is likely to have some effects as a child goes through the grieving process, but a sudden, violent death—especially if witnessed by the child—can add serious trauma to the grief.

Not only does the child suffer acute loss with the death of a parent, but the child is likely to experience disruption of his or her whole life. Living situations may change, and there's bound to be some interruption of the daily routines. The accompanying stress can affect not only the child's behavior but also his or her development. According to Alicia Lieberman and her coauthors (2003), "When an attachment figure dies, the child loses intimate patterns of interaction that organize key developmental domains and constitute the building blocks for the child's sense of self" (p. 10). If there is a surviving parent, that person may be unavailable to give emotional support to the child because of his or her own grieving and adjusting to the changing life circumstances.

The nature of the death also influences the reactions. Some deaths can represent social stigma—for example, dying from AIDS, being murdered while in prison, or committing suicide. Those deaths are quite different from parents who die in the line of duty, such as members of the military, police officers, or firefighters. Their survivors may have conflicting emotions. Seeing loved ones as heroes deserving gratitude can mix pride with grief. But survivors can also experience resentment that the loved one chose service over family duties and died for that choice.

WHAT TEACHERS CAN DO

- Realize that death, and the meanings, behaviors, words, symbols, and beliefs associated with it, are all highly cultural and vary greatly from one group to another. You may never know in depth what a death means to a family—unless you were part of an anthropological study, which as a teacher you aren't. Just know that there will be things you don't understand in your attempts to support this child and family.

- Anticipate that there may be behavioral changes in the child whose parent died. It helps to understand that these behaviors and the feelings behind them are mourning responses. Be prepared for crying, anger, fears, anxiety, frustration, increased aggression, and possible regression.

- Keep things as familiar as possible for the child. Teachers and other early care and education professionals can provide a dependable, stable environment with predictable routines, which may be a contrast to what the child is getting at home.

- Give the child emotional support through all the stages of grieving. These include: 1) hoping the lost parent will return, and then finally giving up that hope; 2) integrating the memories of the parent into an ongoing sense of self; and 3) turning to another attachment figure to find emotional bonds (Lieberman, Compton, Van Horn, & Ippen, 2003, p. 7).

- Recognize that children's behaviors, such as protesting, emotional withdrawal, anger, and aggression, that are aimed at you are grief responses. Don't take them personally.

- Allow children to work out their feelings in play. Not only does the grieving child need opportunities to express feelings through words or play, the other children may also be feeling anxious.

- Be aware that holidays, when many programs have children make cards and presents for their parents, may be hard on the child in mourning. Consider expanding the activities to include a wide variety of significant others in each child's life. Be especially available to the bereaved child during these activities.

- Recognize the grief in the other adults in the family, and do what you can to support them emotionally.

- Pay attention to your own feelings. Death affects everyone, and you are no exception. You have your own issues and history. Separate those from the present circumstances in this family.

- If appropriate, get the surviving family members connected to other parents in the program so that they can get additional support.

- Don't try to be a therapist or a savior, but do support the parents in accessing resources. If the child or family needs therapy, help them find a referral.

Anticipate that there may be some behavioral changes in a child when a death in the family occurs. It helps to understand that these behaviors are mourning responses.

46

Finding Community Resources and Making Referrals

When schools and other early care and education programs focus on the sharing of information and resources, everybody benefits. It isn't just the professionals who have information—families have their own resources that they can share with staff and other families. A sharing spirit makes the difference between a program in which the staff gives and the families receive and one in which the giving and receiving are reciprocal. The latter kind of program becomes a community. The problem is that this doesn't happen easily. The professionals are busy with the children, and when it comes to resources, they are lucky if they have even a resource list to give out.

A huge question arises with low-income and homeless families. How can teachers and caregivers create partnerships with parents and expect them to be part of their children's care and education if the family's basic needs, such as food, clothing, and shelter, are not being met? Families who lack the ability to provide for the basic needs of their children show up in schools and early care and education programs in significant numbers. According to the Children's Defense Fund (2011), the number of children in poverty increased by 950,000 between 2009 and 2010, rising from 15.5 million to 16.4 million. This is more than one in five children in America. Children have suffered more than any other age group during these difficult economic times. Many of the children in schools and early care and education programs come from single-parent families, and some of those children and their family members have disabilities and other kinds of challenges. According to Turnbull and Turnbull (2001), "Those households headed by a single parent who has a child with a developmental disability have the lowest income of any household type" (p. 217).

We won't be able to solve a family's economic problems with the strategies in this chapter, but an understanding about family support services can help teachers, caregivers, and providers direct families to the community resources that can help them. From its early beginning, Head Start recognized the importance of connecting the community to their programs and the families to the community. This federally funded program has long served as a model for other programs.

There are three main federal programs that provide support for low-income families: The federal program designed to provide economic help is called TANF (Temporary Assistance for Needy Families). Social Security provides income assistance for low-income families with children with disabilities under SSI (Supplemental Security Income). Medicaid provides health care insurance for low-income people. Even though

Schools and child care programs are natural meeting places "to bring together the needs of children and families and the community resources that they may need to access" (Seiderman, 2003, p. 358).

they are underfunded, these three programs can begin to address some of the economic and medical needs of low-income families. Some states have programs that help to fill in where federal programs have proved to be insufficient.

WHAT TEACHERS CAN DO

- Your primary role is to support families in accessing resources. Don't diagnose them or provide therapy—those are not part of your job. Check to make sure you aren't coming at your job with a savior mentality.

- Ethel Seiderman (2003), who founded an organization called the Family Services Project, said, "Community building based on caring relationships encourages optimal availability and use of resources. Accessing resources doesn't happen in a vacuum" (p. 360). She offers some strategies for early care and education programs to emphasize family support services:

  - Revise your image of your program to include being part of the economic and human service infrastructure of the community. Network with community leaders.
  - Become known and make your voice heard in your community, including attending school board meetings. Become a speaker at social, business, and professional groups in the community.
  - Partner with various community organizations so that together you are all stronger.

- Turnbull and Turnbull (2001) offer some strategies that early childhood professionals can use in collaboration to improve economic situations for the families they serve:

  - Make sure that the director, teachers, caregivers, and other staff members know about the resources that might help families. These include TANF, the federal Earned Income Tax Credit, state income and other tax credits, food stamps, child support enforcement income, health benefits—Medicaid or the state child health insurance program, and child care subsidies.

- When a program or class includes children with identified or suspected disabilities, make sure someone on the staff knows about early intervention or special education services.
- Team up with other community organizations, such as domestic violence, mental health, and substance abuse agencies, to address prevention and treatment issues for vulnerable families.
- Increase advocacy along with parents and other groups at both state and local levels to do the following:
  - Improve the availability of high-quality child care and education that is responsive to family needs.
  - Promote economic and security supports for families, while working on a shared agenda that is focused on the families with the most severe barriers to getting their economic needs met.

Working with Parents who Constantly Complain

47

WHAT TEACHERS NEED TO KNOW

Here is an example of a complaining parent: *This individual is always in the principal's office with a new criticism or complaint. She used to talk to the teacher but he got tired of it, so he got really busy when she was around. Now she goes to the principal. This is not an uncommon situation.*

Before her child was old enough to go to school, he was in child care. This mother's behavior there was the same. She was always complaining to the staff and went to the director on a regular basis. Staff meetings were regularly taken up with this one mother's complaints. Why all these complaints?

Only when you understand what's going on with this parent can you determine what to do about it. It helps to think about how parents, usually mothers, are responsible for the well-being of their young children, which includes even the most personal aspects of their daily care. When that care is taken out of the parents' hands, such as it is by child care or school, they may feel frustrated that they can't control it, and to some extent don't even know how it is being done. This can weigh heavily on parents when they have the responsibility but are not in charge because they have to delegate it.

Lynet Uttal (2002) made an ethnographic study of mothers who had children in child care arrangements. She found, among other things, that the responsibility for choosing care and education programs for children was left up to mothers, even if fathers or other family members were part of the picture. With responsibility comes the potential for error. The mothers wanted very much to believe that their children were getting high-quality care, but they were worried that perhaps they had made a bad choice and their children were not in the best situation. They exhibited ambivalence in most cases, and it centered on how to monitor and ensure the quality of their arrangements. Worries about safety were high on the list. Programming and staffing were concerns. These mothers constantly wondered about things like what was the relationship like between their child and the professional? What kind of care was their child getting? What if their child cried and nobody paid attention? What caused that bruise on the child's leg? How was the child being disciplined? Or was there no discipline? Those questions weighed heavily on the minds of the women Uttal interviewed.

Of course, every article in the newspaper about suspected abuse in a family child care home or center intensifies the worries. Who is watching out for the children is a question parents and other family members have to ask when their children are in homes and institutions where they can't monitor them very well.

In Uttal's study, how comfortable mothers were about their children's out-of-home experience depended on the relationships they had with their children's care and education professionals. Uttal made it clear that relationships really matter.

The mother in the story that opened this chapter doesn't seem to have had much of a relationship with the staff in child care or later with the teacher in her child's school. It's easy to say it is her own fault, but is it? Whose responsibility is it to build the relationship? In a world where parents may feel like guests at best, and intruders or spies at worst, in their children's school or other care and education settings, it is up to the professionals to help them feel otherwise by working on building a relationship with each one.

So let's look back at the mother who always criticizes and complains. Maybe behind the complaints are worries and frustrations. Maybe she has ambivalent feelings about her child being away from her. Maybe she feels guilty. Are her criticisms and complaints her way of making herself feel like she is taking charge, fulfilling her responsibilities? Maybe she feels like the responsibility for her child is out of her hands and she wants to have more involvement in it, but she doesn't know how to get involved except to be critical of what is going on. In that case, give her more options to be part of things.

A completely different explanation might be that this parent feels she doesn't get enough attention. Maybe the only time anybody listens to her is when she complains. She's like the child who is ignored until he misbehaves. You can't just keep ignoring the child—or the parent, either. They need attention, and they are getting it in a way that works. You have to show them that other ways work, too. Give her recognition when she is not complaining. It may not be easy, but just as we can improve children's behavior by giving them attention at appropriate times, we can do the same with adults.

Another explanation may have to do with diversity and her cultural practices. Is she concerned that the program's practices are not in tune with what she wants for her child? Is she worried about her child's identity formation in a program that isn't supporting who the family is and where it is coming from. Are there bias issues involved?

Take a complaining parent seriously and try to make that parent feel at home in the program.

WHAT TEACHERS CAN DO

- Try to understand what it must be like to be in this mother's position.
- Examine your program, your classroom, and yourself and see if you can discover any bias that you may be overlooking.
- Work on building a relationship with her by initiating contact instead of sending her away when she initiates it. Get to know her. Find a way to spend some time with her when you're not so busy with the children. If you begin to relate to one another differently, her complaining may ease up.
- Take her seriously, and try to make her feel at home in the program.
- Try to get her involved in helping out.
- Introduce her to some other parents.
- Discuss with the principal or director what else can be done.
- Get other staff members involved.
- Practice respectfully maintaining boundaries.
- Get support for yourself, if you need it.

48 Working with Family Members Who Appear Hostile

WHAT TEACHERS NEED TO KNOW

Let's look at a parent who is often angry, aggressive, and seems to harbor deep hostility. This is a parent who presents real challenges to many early childhood professionals. Those of us who work with young children may have a tendency to be nice and want others to be nice as well—that's not true of all of us, but it is an impression one gets when in the field for very long. Teachers, caregivers, and staff who like "nice" may give up on working with what they consider to be a hostile parent. Interestingly enough, most teachers don't give up on children as readily as they do parents. In fact, some teachers energize themselves to take on a challenging child, whereas they want to turn their back on an angry parent. Some even want to run away and hide! Worse, some give up on all parents because of a few difficult experiences.

Diversity may be an issue when someone who appears hostile is expressing him- or herself in ways that may be appropriate in their culture. Sometimes even pitch or tone of voice may be misinterpreted by someone of a different cultural or linguistic background. A person who is not the least bit angry may sound that way without intending to.

Some people who often display hostility have been targets for bias and discrimination all their lives because of race, ethnic origin, or perhaps economic level. Maybe that has been your situation. In such cases, it may help for you to understand where the family member is coming from so that you can better remove barriers to the partnership.

WHAT TEACHERS CAN DO

- Avoid labeling parents or anybody else. Labels can get in the way of your ability to work with others. Labeling and stereotyping go together. Avoid both.

- Examine your own attitudes. What are your biases? Are they entering into this situation?

- Self-reflection may help you discover the role that projection can play when reacting strongly to people. Sometimes the very traits that we dislike in ourselves are the ones that bother us most in other people. That's called projection. Sometimes we've even managed to hide those traits from ourselves. You may be able to communicate better once you do some honest self-reflection.

- Separate your feelings from the parents' feelings, as you do with children. Notice when defensive or aggressive feelings arise in you. Getting angry in the face of another's anger is not usually an effective response if it is a person with whom you are trying to establish a relationship. An experienced professional learns to step aside from a child's anger and not take it personally. Most can acknowledge the feelings without getting caught up in them. Just as we do for children, we can learn to do for adults.

- Most times family members who are angry just need to vent. Listen and reflect back to them what you heard. Work at identifying the problem and seeing if they have a solution.

- Get support for yourself if you need it. Don't go it alone.

- Try to accept the feelings of the person you perceive as hostile and understand them if you can. Don't overanalyze; you aren't a therapist. But do realize that, for example, a parent's strong feelings may relate to genuine concern for her child. She may lack skills for communicating her concerns, so instead of being assertive about what's bothering her, she may use aggression instead. Sometimes people's behavior is the opposite of what they are feeling. People with low self-esteem act conceited, people who feel powerless can become pushy, and people who are afraid may exhibit anger instead.

- Recognize that strong feelings are not usually about whatever triggers them, but have deeper roots. Fear or grief may well show up as anger toward someone who has nothing to do with what makes the person afraid or with the loss they are grieving.

- Your job is to remain calm and work to open up communication by becoming aware of what blocks it; for example:
  - Defensive responses
  - Arguing
  - Criticizing
  - Distracting

- Practice what is called *active listening*—a time-honored strategy used by early childhood educators. Originally designed for use with children, active listening also works well with adults. It is a way of acknowledging feelings so that the other person realizes you are accepting rather than criticizing them or trying to make them go away. Put into nonjudgmental words what you perceive them to be saying, and their feelings behind it. The key is to be precise. If you say, "You seem irritated," and the parent is furious, then you missed the mark. But if he or she corrects you, then at least you've got a start on communication.

- Realize that the time and effort you put into working with an angry parent may result in your meeting up with the nice person underneath the angry cover.

Recognize that strong feelings are not usually about whatever triggers them, but often have deeper roots.

49 Talking with Families About Behavior Changes

WHAT TEACHERS NEED TO KNOW

Let's start with an example. *Todd is having a hard time lately in class. He used to be easygoing and able to get along with everybody, but lately he has changed a good deal. He refuses to comply with the rules. He argues with everybody, including the teacher. He always seems tired, and sometimes he just sits and stares off into space. He has always been a happy, active child, so the change in Todd's behavior has his teacher worried. She wonders if this is a stage he is going through. Maybe something is going on at home. The teacher decides to talk to his mother.*

Talking to his mother is a fine idea, but if the purpose of the conversation is to ask about what is going on at home that would explain the change in Todd's behavior, the teacher should reconsider. This approach to understanding child behavior is so common in early care and education that most professionals don't think twice about it.

Jim Greenman (2003) was an advocate for not prying into a family's private life in the name of understanding the child better. He said, "Respect for parents demands that, unless the situation is one of abuse or neglect, the parents control what information they wish to share" (p. 317). Greenman questioned the idea that teachers have any more right to know about what goes on in the family than the family has a right to know about teachers' private lives. If a teacher is going through a divorce, should a notice go home to the parents to watch for changes in the children's behavior because their teacher is so stressed out? What if the parents were told to be understanding with their children and give them extra attention because of what is going on at school?

If you can see that a child is under stress, do you really need to know why? Will you treat him differently if you know the roots of his stress? Why not just support him and give him what he needs regardless of what is going on at home? Greenman suggests giving flexibility, warmth, and nurturing to the child who is under stress. If Todd, for instance, wants to talk about how he feels, the teacher can listen. And if Todd's parents come to the teacher and want to share what's going on, that's very different from the teacher asking.

The following are some ideas about how to relate to parents when you see a change of behavior in their children.

WHAT TEACHERS CAN DO

- Be a good observer. Be clear about what the changes are and under what circumstances they occur. Record your observations. Be careful to be objective and descriptive.
- Consider whether the child is entering a new developmental phase. If so, the behavior changes may be an indication of that. Sometimes it's just a matter of waiting until a child gets used to whatever he or she is going through.

- Respond to the child's behavior in ways that help her relax, if possible. Let her know she has your support and understanding. Do what you can to meet her needs.

- Look at the classroom and determine whether there has been a change there that is affecting this child's behavior. Is there something you can do about that change? Keep things as predictable as possible.

- If you see that the child is feeling pressure in the classroom, do what you can to ease that pressure.

- Set and keep limits for the child, but do so in calm and gentle ways. See if you can make things easier for the child at school. Meet his needs as best as you can. If you determine that he is feeling pressure in the classroom, ease off.

- If you ask the parent or family member to talk with you about the situation at school, be prepared to share your observations and what you are doing to respond. Report what has worked and what hasn't. Listen to any suggestions about how to work with the behaviors.

- Make sure your observations are reported in nonjudgmental terms. Describe behavior without putting value judgments on it.

- Respect the family's right to privacy. Don't ask what is going on at home. If they choose to share with you what is happening, keep this information confidential. Offer your support and use your best listening skills. Don't offer advice about the parents' situation.

- If the family member hasn't already given you suggestions for how to work with her child in school, ask her, and then listen to her ideas. Give them a try. They just might make a difference.

- You can do all of the above without needing to know if the parents are getting a divorce, the father got laid off or is in jail, there's a new baby in the family (although the parents or the child are likely to share that news with you voluntarily), or grandma just died and grandpa came to live with them. Any one of those situations could cause a change in behavior. You can work with the change without knowing the reason it came about.

Be a good observer so you can be clear about the changes in behavior and under what circumstances they occur. Make sure your observations are reported to the family member in nonjudgmental terms.

50 Referring Families for Abuse or Neglect

Abuse and neglect are heartbreaking conditions for anyone to face, yet every day children who are victims of such treatment come into classrooms and early care and education programs along with their families. Legal definitions of abuse and neglect differ by state, but in general, abuse is characterized by mistreatment that either results in physical harm or is likely to harm the child in some other way. Physical abuse includes spanking only if the child is bruised or injured in some other way. Sexual abuse includes any form of sexual conduct in which children are used to provide sexual gratification for the perpetrator. Also included as sexual abuse are any forms of sexual exploitation, including child pornography. Emotional abuse is harder to see, but it relates to rejection, isolation, or corruption of a child. Terrorizing a child is a form of emotional abuse. And under certain circumstances, even ignoring a child can be considered emotional abuse. Emotional abuse includes such widely ranging examples as allowing a child to engage in criminal activity, inattention to a child's need for psychological help, verbal abuse, and exposing a child to domestic violence. Neglect falls into a different category of abuse and is characterized by refusal to meet basic needs, including withholding affection, attention, or health care.

It may seem as if abuse and neglect happen only among low-income families, but that's not true. Abuse and neglect happen at all levels of society, although maltreatment occurs more often to children who have disabilities. There are some risk factors that should be considered. Certainly, poverty can cause stress, and stress can cause abuse. Isolation of the family from others can be another risk factor. The family's lack of coping skills or anger management skills can contribute to the possibility of abuse. Health issues in the family can result in neglect of a child. Characteristics of the child can be a factor in abuse and neglect as well. When several of these factors work together, the family is more vulnerable. Knowing the families you work with may help you direct some to support services and prevent abuse before it happens.

Anyone who works with young children is a mandated reporter—by law, that person must report any suspected abuse or neglect. You don't have to prove it, just suspect it. If you suspect abuse, be sure you have your facts straight, and have grounds for your suspicions. Don't do anything with the family yourself. Your school or program may have a reporting procedure—an authority to go to as the second step, such as the director, principal, or school social worker. Finally, a call to your local child protection agency to report the abuse is essential.

If families have been referred to your program after having been identified by authorities as having maltreated their children, it is your job to work with them. You may have feelings about their children and what they have been through. Nevertheless, you need to approach these families with the same openness, acceptance, and respect with which you approach any other family. It may be a challenge to do so, but that's what is needed. In the long run, everybody benefits.

WHAT TEACHERS CAN DO

- Becoming aware of your own feelings and attitudes is important. You may feel angry with a parent or family member for an injury inflicted on a child, but your job is to get to know the parent or family member and work to understand, respect, and support him or her.

- Build a trusting relationship with all parents and parent substitutes, including those who have been referred for abuse or neglect. It may be especially difficult because you are a mandated reporter and the family knows that. They may not see you as being "on their side." It is important that you work as hard to relate to them as you do to other parents and family members. One way to show that you are trustworthy is to keep confidentiality. Do not talk about a family to others.

- You may assume that children who have been abused and neglected no longer feel close to their parent(s). Your assumption may be wrong. Attachment usually persists even in extremely abusive circumstances. Be very careful that you do not say anything negative to children about their parents. Show them that you support both them and their parents.

- Help prevent abuse by doing the following:

  - Provide support when needed, or refer to outside sources of support. If parents have been referred to your program because of abuse or neglect, it is likely that they already are connected with a support group. For other families under stress, keep up to date on community resource information. Know the numbers for parenting hotlines, family support centers, crisis centers, parent support groups, Parents Anonymous, and counseling and parent education programs. Preventing abuse and neglect is a much better approach than addressing them after they occur.

This excerpt from a preschool parent handbook is a fairly standard statement about the legal mandate that early care and education professionals have to report suspected child abuse. In some programs, families enrolling their children are required to sign a statement that they understand suspected child abuse will be reported to the authorities.

15

Menus

Monthly menus are posted in the kitchen area in both centers and on the bulletin boards near the entry doors. Menus are available to parents upon request.

Food Allergies

Be sure to notify us of any food allergies. Food allergies are listed on the front of the child's nametag and on lists posted in the children's eating areas and on the refrigerators.

Minor modifications can be made to many of our menus to meet the needs of children with allergies (e.g. burritos with no cheese or white flour tortillas instead of whole wheat). Parents with children with extreme food allergies should ask for menus to determine any day when their child is unable to eat what is being served. On that day, the parent needs to bring a main course item for the child. It should be marked and given to a staff member.

Other Allergies

Pets and regular outside play are parts of our daily curriculum. If your child has an extreme allergy, please let us know.

Child Abuse

All employees of the DVC Developmental Children's Center are mandated to report suspected instances of child abuse, mental suffering or endangerment of the emotional well being of children that they become aware of in their professional capacity, or within the scope of their employment.

We want to work with all of the adults whether they are parents, staff or students associated with our Center to keep children safe and healthy. Additional helpful information is available from the Family Stress Center in Concord (925/827-0212) or the Contra Costa County Child Abuse Prevention Council (925/946-9961).

- Offer ideas for improving parenting skills, such as using problem-solving strategies for child guidance, rather than physical punishment.
- Model nonviolent and nonaggressive approaches to conflict resolution in the classroom with the children.
- Work with children who lack social skills to improve them. Some child behaviors put them at risk for being abused in families that have other risk factors as well.

References

Allen, J. (2007). *Creating welcoming schools: A practical guide to home-school partnerships with diverse families*. New York: Teachers College Press.

American Academy of Family Physicians. (2003). *Definition of Family*. Retrieved January 15, 2009, from http://www.aafp.org/online/en/home/policy/policies/f/familydefinitionof.html.

American Psychological Association Online. (2004). *What is sexual orientation?* Retrieved February 10, 2009, from http://www.apa.org/pubinfo/answers.html.

Anderson, S., & Sabatelli, R. (2007). *Family interaction: A multigenerational perspective* (4th ed.). Boston: Allyn & Bacon.

Baker, A. C., & Manfredi-Petitt, L. A. (2004). *Relationships, the heart of quality care: Creating community among adults in early care settings*. Washington, DC: National Association for the Education of Young Children.

Balaban, N. (2006). *Everyday goodbyes: Starting school and early care, a guide to the separation process*. New York: Teachers College Press.

Ballenger, C. (1992, Summer). Because you like us: The language of control. *Harvard Educational Review, 62*(2), 199–208.

Barrera, I., & Corso, R. (2003). *Skilled dialogue*. Baltimore, MD: Brookes.

Basso, K. (2007). To give up on words: Silence in Western Apache culture. In L. Monaghan & J. E. Goodman (Eds.), *A cultural approach to interpersonal communication* (pp. 77–87). Malden, MA: Blackwell.

Bead, C. (2011, March/April). The importance of fathers in the lives of their children. *Exchange, 33*(2, Serial No. 198), 52–54.

Bennett, T. (2007). *Mapping family resources and support: Spotlight on young children and families*. Washington, DC: National Association for the Education of Young Children.

Bisson, J. (2002). *Celebrate: An antibias guide to enjoying holidays in early childhood programs*. St. Paul, MN: Redleaf Press.

Bisson, J. (2008). Holiday lessons learned in an early childhood classroom. In A. Pelo (Ed.), *Rethinking early childhood education* (pp. 165–170). Milwaukee, WI: Rethinking Schools.

Bloom, P. J., Eisenberg, P., & Eisenberg, E. (2003, Spring/Summer). Reshaping early childhood programs to be more family responsive. *America's Family Support Magazine*, 36–38.

Bodrova, E. and Leong, D. J. (2007). *Tools of the mind: The Vygotsky approach to early childhood education* (2nd ed.). Upper Saddle River, NJ: Pearson/Merrill Prentice Hall.

Brand, S. (1996, January). Making parent involvement a reality: Helping teachers develop partnerships with parents. *Young Children, 51*(2), 76–81.

Brault, L., & Brault, T. (2005). *Children with challenging behavior*. Phoenix, AZ: CPG Publishing.

Brault, L. M. V. (2007). *Making inclusion work: Strategies to promote belonging for children with special needs in child care settings*. Sacramento, CA: California Department of Education.

Bravo, E. (2008). It's all of our business: What fighting for family-friendly policies could mean for early childhood educators. In A. Pelo (Ed.), *Rethinking early childhood education* (pp. 197–200). Milwaukee, WI: Rethinking Schools.

Bredekamp, S. (2003). Resolving contradictions between cultural practices. In C. Copple (Ed.), *A world of difference*. Washington, DC: National Association for the Education of Young Children.

Bredekamp, S., & Copple, C. (1997). *Developmentally appropriate practice in early childhood programs* (2nd ed.). Washington, DC: National Association for the Education of Young Children.

Brooks, D. (2011, April). *The social animal: A story of how success happens*. London: Short Books.

Bruno, H. E. (2005, September). At the end of the day: Policies, procedures and practices to ensure smooth transitions. *Exchange, 16*, 66–69.

Burchinal, M., Jurgens, J., & Roberts, J. (2005). The role of home literacy practices and preschool children's language and emergent literacy skills. *Journal of Speech, Language, and Hearing Research, 48*(2), 345–59.

Caldwell, B. (2003). Advocacy is everybody's business. In B. Neugebauer & R. Neugebauer (Eds.), *The art of leadership* (pp. 46–48). Redmond, WA: Exchange Press.

Cappola, J. (2005). English language learners: Language and literacy development during the preschool years. *New England Reading Association Journal, 41*(2), 18–23.

Carroll, K. 2007. *A guide to great field trips*. Chicago: Zephyr.

Caspe, M. (2003). *Family literacy: A review of programs and critical perspectives*. Cambridge, MA: Harvard Family research Project.

Casper, V. (2003). Very young children in lesbian- and gay-headed families: Moving beyond acceptance. *Zero to Three, 23*(3), 18–26.

Chao, R. (1994). Beyond parental control and authoritarian parenting style: Understanding Chinese parenting through the cultural notion of training. *Child Development, 65*, 1111–1119.

Charmian, K. (2007). Childhood bilingualism: Research on infancy through school age. *Literacy, 41*(2), 110–111.

Children's Defense Fund. (2011). *The state of America's children*. Washington, DC.

Clay, J. (2004). Creating safe, just places to learn for children of lesbian and gay parents: The NAEYC Code of Ethics in action. *Young Children, 59*(6), 34–38.

Cohen, B. (2008, July/August). Communicating with parents about food allergies. *Exchange, 182*, 61–65.

Colabucci, L., & Conley, M. D. (2008). What makes a family: Representations of adoption in children's literature. In T. Turner-Vorbeck & M. M. Marsh (Eds.), *Other kinds of families: Embracing diversity in schools* (pp. 139–160). New York: Teachers College Press.

Copple, C., & Bredekamp, S. (2009) *Developmentally appropriate practice in early childhood programs serving children birth through age 8* (3rd ed.). Washington, DC: National Association for the Education of Young Children.

Copple, C., Bredekamp, S., & Gonzalez-Mena, J. (2011). *Basics of sdevelopmentally appropriate practice: An introduction for teachers of infants and toddlers*. Washington, DC: National Association for Education of Young Children.

Council on Interracial Books for Children. (2008). 10 quick ways to analyze children's books for racism and sexism. In A. Pelo (Ed.), *Rethinking early childhood education* (pp. 211–214), Milwaukee, WI: Rethinking Schools.

Covey, S. R. (2012). Foreword. In K. Patterson, J. Grenny, R. McMillan, & A. Switzler, *Crucial conversations* (pp. xi–xv). New York: McGraw-Hill.

Dowhey, M. (2008). Heather's moms got married. In A. Pelo (Ed.), *Rethinking early childhood education* (pp. 177–179). Milwaukee, WI: Rethinking Schools.

Curtis, D., & Carter, M. (2003). *Designs for living and learning*. St. Paul, MN: Redleaf Press.

Daper, L., & Duffy, B. (2001). Working with parents. In G. Pugh (Ed.), *Contemporary issues in the early years: Working collaboratively for children*. London: Paul Chapman Publishing.

Darragh, J. (2008, July/August). Access and inclusion: Ensuring engagement in EC environments. *Exchange, 182*, 20–23.

Derman-Sparks, L. (2008). Why an antibias curriculum? In A. Pelo (Ed.), *Rethinking early childhood education* (pp. 7–12). Milwaukee, WI: Rethinking Schools.

Derman-Sparks, L. (2011, July/August). Anti-bias education. *Exchange. 33*(4, Serial No. 200), 55–58.

Derman-Sparks, L., & Olsen Edwards, J. (2010) *Anti-bias education for ourselves and others.* Washington, DC: National Association for the Education of Young Children.

DeVol, P. E., Payne, R. K., & Smith, T. D. (2002) Bridges out of poverty: Strategies for professionals and communities (revised edition). Highlands, TX: Process, Inc.

DeWeese-Parkinson, C. (2008). Talking the talk: Integrating indigenous languages into a Head Start classroom. In A. Pelo (Ed.), *Rethinking early childhood education* (pp. 175–176). Milwaukee, WI: Rethinking Schools.

Diffily, D. (2001, Summer). Family meetings: Teachers and families build relationships. *Dimensions of Early Childhood*, 5–9.

DiNatale, L. (2002, September). Developing high-quality family involvement programs in early childhood settings. *Young Children, 57*(5), 90–95.

Donohue, C. (2010 September/October). There's an app for (almost) everything: New technology tools for early childhood professionals – Part 2. *Exchange, Serial No. 195*, 78–82.

Dubosarky, M., Murphy, B., Roehrig, G., Frost, L. C., Jones, J.,. . . Bement, J. (2011, September). Animosh tracks on the playground, minnows in the sensory table: Incorporating cultural themes to promote preschoolers' critical thinking in American Indian Head Start classrooms. *Young Children. 66*(5), 20–29.

Edelman, M. W. (2003, October 19). Children in America: A report card. Interview in *Parade Magazine*, p. 13.

Eggers-Pierola, C. (2005). *Connections and commitments: A Latino-based framework for early childhood educators.* Portsmouth, NH: Heinemann.

Ehrlich, B. (n.d.) Look who's blogging [STATS]. *Social Media News and Web Tips – Mashable – The Social Media Guide.* Retrieved July 27, 2010, from http://mashable.com/2010/06/04/look-whos-blogging-stats/.

Eisaguirre, L. (2007). *Stop pissing me off!* Cincinnati, OH: Adams Media.

Ellison, S. (2009). *Taking the war out of our words: The art of powerful nondefensive communication* (4th ed.). Deadwood, OR: Wyatt MacKensie.

Epstein, J. L. (2001). *School, family, and community partnerships: Preparing educators and improving schools.* Boulder, CO: Westview.

Epstein, J. L. (Ed.). (2008). *School, family, and community partnerships: Your handbook for action* (3rd ed.). Los Angeles: Corwin.

Fernandez, M. T., & Marfo, K. (2005). Enhancing infant-toddler adjustment during transitions to care. *Zero to Three, 26,* 41–48.

Fitzgerald, D. (2004). *Parent partnership in the early years.* London: Continuum.

Galinsky, E. (2010). *Mind in the making: The seven essential life skills every child needs.* New York: HarperCollins.

Garner, A. (2004). *Families like mine: Children of gay parents tell it like it is.* New York: HarperCollins Publishers.

Gartrell, D. (2004). *The power of guidance.* Washington, DC: National Association for the Education of Young Children.

Geelen, A. (2009, January). Investigating nature in New Zealand. *Wonder: Tawa Montessori School strives for "hundred-acre wood" in the backyard, 1*(2), 1–3.

Gelnaw, A., Brickley, M., Marsh, H., & Ryan, D. (2004). *Opening doors: Lesbian and gay parents and schools.* Washington, DC: Family Pride Coalition.

Gestwicki, C. (2004). *Home, school, and community relations: A guide to working with parents.* Albany, NY: Thompson Delmar.

Gies, E. (2008, Fall/Winter). Playing it smart! *Land and People, 20*(2), 24–31.

Goldberg, R. J., Haugen, K., Sivanathan, A., & Spakota, R. D. (2011, September/October). World forum working group report on inclusion. *Exchange, 33*(55, Serial No. 201), 56.

Gonzalez, J. E., Uhing, B. M. (2008). Home literacy environment and young Hispanic children's English and Spanish oral language: A communality analysis. *Journal of Early Intervention, 30*(2), 116–39.

Gonzalez-Mena, J. (2002, January/February). Personal power: Creating new realities. *Child Care Information Exchange, 143*, 59–62.

Gonzalez-Mena, J. (2004, September). What can an orphanage teach us? Lessons from Budapest. *Young Children, 60*(5), 26–29.

Gonzalez-Mena, J. (2007, May/June). Thinking about thinking: How can I get inside your head? *Exchange, 175*, 50–52.

Gonzalez-Mena, J. (2008a). *Diversity in early care and education: Honoring differences* (5th ed.). New York: McGraw-Hill.

Gonzalez-Mena, J. (2008b). *Foundations of early childhood education in a diverse society* (4th ed.). New York: McGraw-Hill.

Gonzalez-Mena, J. (2012). *Child, family and community: Family-centered early care and Education.* Upper Saddle River, NJ: Pearson.

Gonzalez-Mena, J., & Eyer, D. (2012. *Infants, toddlers, and caregivers* (9th ed) New York: McGraw-Hill.

Gonzalez-Mena, J., & Shareef, I. (2005, November). Discussing diverse perspectives on guidance. *Young Children, 60*(6), 34–38.

Gonzalez-Mena, J., & Stonehouse, A. (2003, July/August). High-maintenance parent or parent partner? Working with a parent's concern. *Child Care Information Exchange,* 16–18.

Gonzalez-Mena, J., & Stonehouse, A. (2008). *Making links: A collaborative approach to planning and practice in early childhood programs* (American ed.). New York: Teachers College Press.

Greenman, J. (2003). Places for childhood include parents too. In B. Neugebauer & R. Neugebauer (Eds.), *The art of leadership.* Redmond, WA: Exchange Press.

Greenman, J., Schweikert, G., & Stonehouse, A. (2008). *Prime times: A handbook for excellence in infant and toddler programs* (2nd ed.). St. Paul, MN: Readleaf Press.

Greenman, M. (2011, March/April). The family partnership. *Exchange, 33*(2, Serial No.198), 46–8.

Grefsrud, S. (2011, March/April). Room at the table: Parent engagement in Head Start. *Exchange, 33*(2, Serial No. 198), 57–59.

Haight, W. L., & Carter-Black, J. (2004). His eyes on the sparrow: Teaching and learning in an African American church. In E.Gregory, S. Long, & D. Volk (Eds.), *Many pathways to literacy: Young children learning with siblings, grandparents, peers and communities* (pp.195–207). London: Routledge.

Hale-Benson, J. (1986). *Black children: Their roots, culture and learning styles.* Baltimore, MD: Johns Hopkins University Press.

Hall, E. T. (1981). *Beyond culture.* Garden City, NY: Anchor Press/Doubleday.

Hall, E. T. (1959). *The silent language.* New York: Fawcett.

Haynes-Lawrence, D. (2009, January/February). Crisis nurseries: Emergency services for children and families in need. *Exchange, 185*, 16–20.

Healy, J. (2008). Cybertots: Technology and the preschool child. In A. Pelo (Ed.), *Rethinking early childhood education* (pp. 75–84). Milwaukee, WI: Rethinking Schools.

Healy, J. M. (2011, March/April). Brain readiness: Impacting readiness – Nature and nurture. *Exchange, 33*(2, Serial No. 198), 18–21.

Hernandez, L., & Smith, C. J. (2009, January/February). Disarming cantankerous people: Coping with difficult personalities in the ECE work settings. *Exchange, 185*, 12–14.

Hillman, C. B. (2011, November/December). Home visits: Building relationships by revisiting home visits. *Exchange, 33*(6, Serial No. 202), 80–85.

Hird, J. (2010, January, 29). 20+ mind-blowing social media statistics revisited, Econsultancy, *Community of digital marketing and ecommerce professionals.* Retrieved July, 27, 2010, from http://econsultancy.com/blog/5324-20+mind-blowing-social-media-statistics-revisited.

Hooks, b. (2003). *Rock my soul: Black people and self-esteem.* New York: Atria.

Horn, W., & Sylvester, T. (2005). *Father facts* (4th ed.). Germantown, MD: National Fatherhood Initiative.

Hudson, R. A. (2007). Speech communities. In L. Monaghan & J.E. Goodman (Eds.), *A cultural approach to interpersonal communication* (pp. 212–217). Malden, MA: Blackwell.

Jacobson, T. (2003). *Confronting our discomfort: Clearing the way for antibias in early childhood.* Portsmouth, NH: Heinemann.

Jones, E. (2007). *Teaching adults revisited: Active learning for early childhood educators.* Washington, DC: National Association for the Education of Young Children.

Jones, E., & Cooper, R. (2006). *Playing to get smart*. New York: Teachers College Press.

Kaiser, B., & Rasminsky, J. S. (2003). *Challenging behavior in young children: Understanding, preventing, and responding effectively*. Boston: Allyn and Bacon.

Keeler, R. (2009, January/February). A spring playscape project: Building a tree circle. *Exchange, 185*, 70–71.

Kelley, S., & Whitley, D. (2007). *Grandparents raising grandchildren: A call to action*. Washington, DC: U.S. Census Bureau.

Kitayama, S., Markus, H., & Matsumoto, H. (1995). Culture, self, and emotion: A cultural perspective on "self-conscious" emotions. In J. P. Tangeny & K. W. Fischer (Eds.), *Self-conscious emotions: The psychology of shame, guilt, embarrassment, and pride*. New York: Guilford Press.

Klug, B. (2011). Daring to teach: Challenging the Western narrative of the American Indians in the classroom. In J. Landsman (Ed.), *White teachers/Diverse classrooms* (2nd ed.). Sterling, VA: Stylus.

Kreidler, W. J., & Whitall, S. (2003). Resolving conflict. In C. Copple (Ed.), *A world of difference: Readings on teaching children in a diverse society* (pp. 52–56). Washington, DC: National Association for the Education of Young Children.

Kroeger, J. (2008). Doing the difficult: Schools and lesbian, gay, bisexual, transgendered, and queer families. In T. Turner-Vorbeck & M. M. Marsh (Eds.), *Other kinds of families: Embracing diversity in schools* (pp. 121–138). New York: Teachers College Press.

Kuby, C. R. (2011, September). Humpty Dumpty and Rosa Parks: Making space for critical dialogue with 5- and 6-year-olds. *Young Children. 66*(5), 36–43.

Lee, L. (2004). *Stronger together: Family support and early childhood education*. San Rafael, CA: Parent Services Project.

Lesser, L. K., Burt, T., & Glenaw, A. (2005). *Making room in the circle: Lesbian, gay, bisexual and transgender families in early childhood settings*. San Rafael, CA: Parent Services Project.

Levine, J. A. (1993a). *Getting men involved: Strategies for early childhood programs*. New York: Scholastic.

Levine, J. A. (1993b). Involving gathers in Head Start: A framework for public policy and program development. *Families in Society, 74*(1), 4–19.

Lieberman, A. F., Compton, N. C., Van Horn, P., & Ippen, C. G. (2003). *Losing a parent to death in the early years*. Washington, DC: Zero to Three.

Logue, M. E., Shelton, H. Cronkite, D., & Austin, J. (2007, March). Family ties: Strengthening partnerships with families through toddlers' stories. *Young Children, 62*(2), 85–87.

Lopez, E. J., Salas, L., & Flores, J. P. (2005, November). Hispanic preschool children: What about assessment and intervention? *Young Children, 60*(6), 48–54.

Louv, R. (2008a). Don't know much bout natural history: Education as a barrier to nature. In A. Pelo (Ed.), *Rethinking early childhood education* (pp. 133–136). Milwaukee WI: Rethinking Schools.

Louv, R. (2008b). *Last child in the woods: Saving our children from nature-deficit disorder*. Chapel Hill, NC: Algonquin Books of Chapel Hill.

Maltz, D. N., & Borker, R. A. (2007). A cultural approach to male-female miscommunication. In L. Monaghan & J. E. Goodman (Eds.), *A cultural approach to interpersonal communication* (pp. 77–87). Malden, MA: Blackwell.

Marks, I. (2008). Wards of wisdom: Foster youth on a path toward postsecondary education. In T. Turner-Vorbeck & M. M. Marsh (Eds.), *Other kinds of families: Embracing diversity in schools* (pp. 81–102). New York: Teachers College Press.

Martin, J. (2009, January/February). Using the principles of intentional teaching to communicate effectively with parents. *Exchange, 185*, 53–56.

Maschinot, B. (2008). *The changing face of the United States: The influence of culture on child development*. Washington, DC: Zero to Three.

McDermont, L. B. (2011, September). Play school: Where children and families learn and grow together. *Young Children. 66*(5), 81–86.

McGinnis, M. H., Getskow, V., & Dicker, B. S. (2012, March/April). Parental rights and authorization: Parental rights and release authorization. *Exchange, 34*(2, Serial No. 204), 16–18.

McWilliams, S. M., Maldonado-Mancebo, T., Szczpaniak, P. S., & Jones, J. (2011, November). Supporting native Indian preschoolers and their families: Family-school-community partnerships. *Young Children, 66*(6), 34–41.

Meisels, S. J., & Atkins-Burnett, S. (2005). *Developmental screening in early childhood*. Washington, DC: National Association for the Education of Young Children.

Men in Education Network (MEN) Interest Forum. (2011, September). On our minds. Men in teaching: Gender equality through the promise of gender balance. *Young Children. 66*(5), 64–66.

Milagros Santos, R., Fetting, A., Shaffer, S. (2011, September). Helping families connect literacy with social-emotional development. *Young Children, 66*(5), 88–93.

Miller, K. (2005). *Simple transitions for infants and toddlers*. Beltsville, MD: Gryphon House.

Moerman, M. (2007). Talking culture: Ethnography and conversation analysis. In L. Monaghan & J. E. Goodman (Eds.), *A cultural approach to interpersonal communication* (pp. 119–127). Malden, MA: Blackwell.

Monaghan, L. (2007). Conversations: The link between words and the world. In L. Monaghan & J. E. Goodman (Eds.), *A cultural approach to interpersonal communication* (pp. 145–149). Malden, MA: Blackwell.

Monaghan, L., & Goodman, J. E. (Eds.). (2007). *A cultural approach to interpersonal communication*. Malden, MA: Blackwell.

National Education Association (NEA). (2010). *NEA focus on American Indians and Alaska natives: Charting a new course on native education, focus on 2010–2011*. From www.nea.org/assests/docs/AlAnfocus2010-2011.pdf.

Negri-Pool, L. L. (2008). Welcoming Kalenna: Making our students feel at home. In A. Pelo (Ed.), *Rethinking early childhood education* (pp. 161–169). Milwaukee, WI: Rethinking Schools.

Neubauer, B. (2009, July/August). Celebrating Mother Nature. *Exchange, 182*, 18–19.

Neugebauer, A. (2010, July/August). Going green: Revisiting the power of the individuals. *Exchange, 32*(4, Serial No. 194), 72–3.

North, M., Durekas, T., Siegel, B., & Sisbarro, A. (2009, January/February). The ins and outs of transporting children on field trips. *Exchange, 185*, 84–85.

Nyman, S. I. (2003). Mentoring advocates in the context of early childhood education. In B. Neugebauer & R. Neugebauer (Eds.), *The art of leadership* (pp. 54–57). Redmond, WA: Exchange Press.

Olds, J., & Schwartz, R. S. (2009). *The lonely American: Drifting apart in the twenty-first century*. Boston: Beacon Press.

Olson, M. (2007, March). Strengthening families: Community strategies that work. *Young Children, 62*(2), 26–32.

Palmer, P. (1997). *The courage to teach*. San Francisco: Jossey-Bass.

Parent Services Project (PSP). (2001). *Working together for children and families* [Brochure]. San Rafael, CA.

Parlakian, R. (2001). *The power of question: Building quality relationships with families* [Brochure]. Washington, DC: Zero to Three.

Pelo, A. (2008) A pedagogy for ecology. In A. Pelo (Ed.), *Rethinking early childhood education* (pp. 123–130). Milwaukee, WI: Rethinking Schools.

Pelo, A. (2008). Bringing the lives of lesbian and gay people into our programs. In A. Pelo (Ed.), *Rethinking early childhood education* (pp. 180–182). Milwaukee, WI: Rethinking Schools.

Pelo, A. (Ed.). (2008). *Rethinking early childhood education*. Milwaukee WI: Rethinking Schools.

Perry, B. (2006). Applying principles of neurodevelopment to clinical work with maltreated and traumatized children. In N. B. Webb (Ed.), *Working with traumatized youth in child welfare* (pp. 27–52). New York: Guilford Press.

Perry, G. (2011, March). New books. [Transitions for young children: Creating connections across early childhood systems]. *Young Children, 2*(66), 104.

Petrie, S., & Owen, S. (2005). Authentic relationships in group care for infants and toddlers: Resources for Infant Educarers (RIE) principles into practice. London: Jessica Kingsley Publishers.

Phillips, C. B. (1995). Culture: A process that empowers, In Magione, P, (Ed.), *Infant/Toddler Caregiving: A Guide to Culturally Sensitive Care* (pp. 2–9). Sacramento, CA: California Department of Education and WestEd.

Pollan, M. (2008). *In defense of food*. New York: Penguin Press.

Pope, J., & Seiderman, E. (2001, Winter). The childcare connection. *Family Support, 19*(4), 24–35.

Prieto, H. V. (2009, January). One language, two languages, three languages … more? *Young Children, 64*(1), 52–53.

Ramirez, A. Y. (2008). Immigrant families and schools: The need for a better relationship. In T. Turner-Vorbeck & M. M. Marsh (Eds.), *Other kinds of families: Embracing diversity in schools* (pp. 28–45). New York: Teachers College Press.

Ramirez, C. (2008). Strawberry Fields Forever? An early childhood teacher draws on her past to teach children of migrant farmworkers. In A. Pelo (Ed.), *Rethinking early childhood education* (pp. 171–174). Milwaukee, WI: Rethinking Schools.

Reich, K., & Sylvester K. (2002). *Making fathers count: Assessing the progress of responsible fatherhood efforts.* Baltimore, MD: Annie E. Casey Foundation.

Rieger, L. (2008). A welcoming tone in the classroom: Developing the potential of diverse students and their families. In T. Turner-Vorbeck & M. M. Marsh (Eds.), *Other kinds of families: Embracing diversity in schools* (pp. 64–79). New York: Teachers College Press.

Riojas-Cortez, M. (2011, September). Culture, play, and family: Supporting young children on the autism spectrum. *Young Children. 66*(5), 94–99.

Rishel, T. J. (2008). From the principal's desk: Making the school environment more inclusive. In T. Turner-Vorbeck & M. M. Marsh (Eds.), *Other kinds of families: embracing diversity in schools* (pp. 46–63). New York: Teachers College Press.

Ritter, J. (2007, March). Tips for starting a successful community partnership. *Young Children, 62*(2), 38–40.

Roberts, J. J. & Burchinal, M. (2005). The role of home literacy practices and preschool children's languages and emergent literacy skills. *Journals of Speech, Language, and Hearing Research, 48*(2), 345–59.

Robinson, A., & Stark, D. R. (2002). *Advocates in action: Making a difference for young children.* Washington, DC: National Association for the Education of Young Children.

Rogoff, B. (2003). *The cultural nature of human development.* New York: Oxford University Press.

Rosenkoetter, S., & Knapp-Philo, J. (Eds.). (2006). *Learning to read the world: Language and literacy in the first three years.* Washington, DC: Zero to Three.

Rothstein-Fisch, C. (2003). *Bridging cultures: Teacher education module.* Mahwah, NJ: Erlbaum.

Russell, G. M. (2004). Surviving and thriving in the midst of antigay politics. *The Policy Journal of the Institute for Gay and Lesbian Strategic Studies, 7*(20), 1–7.

Seiderman, E. (2003). Putting all the players on the same page: Accessing resources for the child and family. In B. Neugebauer & R. Neugebauer (Eds.), *The art of leadership* (pp. 58–60). Redmond, WA: Exchange Press.

Shonkoff, J., & Phillips, D. (Eds.). (2000). *From neurons to neighborhoods: The science of early childhood development.* Washington, DC: National Academy Press.

Simon, F. (2011, September/October). Social media: Everyone is doing it! Managing social media in the early childhood ecosystem. *Exchange, 33*(5, Serial No. 201), 12–16.

Simons, K. A., & Curtis, P. A. (2007, March). Connecting with communities: Four successful schools. *Young Children, 62*(2), 12–20.

Snowden, L. J. (1984). *Towards evaluation of black psycho social-competence* in Stanley, S. and Thom Moore, (Eds.). *The Pluralistic Society,* New York: Human Sciences Press.

Social networking/Pew Research Center's Internet & American Life Project. (n.d.). Retrieved July 27, 2010, from http://pewinternet.org/topics/Social-Networking.aspx?typeFilter=5.

Souto-Manning, M. (2010, March). Family involvement: Challenges to consider, strengths to build on. *Young Children, 65*(2), 82–89.

Stephens, K. (2010, July/August). Parent relationships: Building relationships – What parents can teach us about their children. *Exchange, 32*(4, Serial No. 194), 38–40.

Stonehouse, A. (2011, March/April). Moving from family participation to partnerships: Not always easy; always worth the effort. *Exchange, 33*(2, Serial No. 198), 48–51.

Stroll, J., Hamilton, A., Oxley, E., Eastman, A. M, & Brent, R. (March, 2012). Young thinkers in motion: Problem solving and physics in preschool. *Young Children. 67*(2), 20–26.

Sullivan, D. (2010). *Learning to lead.* St. Paul, MN: Redleaf Press.

Tabors, P. O. (2008). One child, two languages (2nd ed.). Baltimore, MD: Brookes.

Tannen, D. (2007). Conversational signals and devices. In L. Monaghan, & J. E. Goodman (Eds.), *A cultural approach to interpersonal communication* (pp. 150–160). Malden, MA: Blackwell.

Thaxton, S. M. (2003). Grandparents as parents: Understanding the issues. In B. Neugebauer & R. Neugebauer (Eds.), *The art of leadership* (pp. 323–325). Redmond, WA: Exchange Press.

Thoennes, T. (2008). Emerging faces of homelessness: Young children, their families, and schooling. In T. Turner-Vorbeck & M. M. Marsh (Eds.), *Other kinds of families: Embracing diversity in schools* (pp. 162–176). New York: Teachers College Press.

Tobaissen, D. P., & Gonzalez-Mena, J. (1998). *A place to begin: Working with parents on issues of diversity.* Oakland, CA: California Tomorrow.

Trumbull, E., Diaz-Meza, R., Hasan, A., & Rothstein-Fisch, C. (2001). *Five-year report of the Bridging Cultures Project: 1996–2000.* San Francisco: WestEd. Retrieved January 28, 2005, from http://www.WestEd.org/BridgingCultures.

Trumbull, E., & Farr, B. (2005). *Language and learning: What teachers need to know.* Norwood, MA: Christopher-Gordon.

Turnbull, A., & Turnbull, R. (2001). *Families, professionals, and exceptionality: Collaborating for empowerment* (4th ed.). Upper Saddle River, NJ: Merrill/Prentice Hall.

Turner-Vorbeck, T., & Marsh, M. M. (2008). *Other kinds of families: Embracing diversity in schools.* New York: Teachers College Press.

Unell, B. C., & Wyckoff, J. L. (2000). *The eight seasons of parenthood. How the stages of parenting constantly reshape our adult identities.* New York: Time Books.

United States Department of Heath and Human Services (U.S. DHHS). (2008). *Child developmental services during home visits and socializations in the early Head Start home-based programs.* From www.headstartinfo.org/pdf/Child_Develpment.pdf.

Uttal, L. (2002). *Making care work: Employed mothers in the new childcare market.* New Brunswick, NJ: Rutgers University Press.

Vygotsky, L. (1978). *Mind in society: The development of higher psychological processes.* Translated by Cole, M. Boston: Harvard University Press.

Warren, C. (n.d.). Moms on Facebook are savvy to marketers [STATS]. *Social Media News and Web Tips – Mashable – The Social Media Guide.* Retrieved July 27, 2010, from http://mashable.com/2010/02/05/moms-on-facebook/.

Wee, W. (2010, March 19). The social media age distribution [STATS]. Retrieved July 27, 2010, from www.penn-olson.com.2010/02/19/the social-media-age-distribution-stats/.

Wood, K., & Youcha, V. (2009). *The ABC's of the ADA: Your early childhood program guide to the American's with Disabilities Act.* Baltimore: Brookes.

Woolum, K. (2011, March/April). Taking your time with families. *Exchange, 33*(2, Serial No. 198), 55–56.

Yoshida, H. (2008, November). The cognitive consequences of early bilingualism. *Zero to Three, 29*(2), 26–30.

Zepeda, M., Gonzalez-Mena, J., Rothstein-Fisch, C., & Trumbull, E. (2006). *Bridging cultures in early care and education: A training module.* Mahwah, NJ: Erlbaum.

Index